Herbert S.
Dickens S.
Pitt

Hack

Conway St.

Thomas
S.

Amelia S.
Charlotte S.

Marlborough Gates

Gloucester S.

Old Convict Prison

Trinity Ch.
Anchorgate Rd.

Nile S.
Unicorn Road

Royal
Naval
Barracks

Alfred Rd.

R.C.
Cathedral
Road

Arundel
S.

Surrey S.

Station

Unicorn
Cross
Daniel S.
King S.
Northm.
St.James York Pl.
Bishop S.

Edinburgh
Garrison
Hosp.

Empire Music
Hall

Victoria

Portsmouth Tn.
Park

Town

Goods St

TSEA

Queen Str.
Union S.
Hanover S.
Albion S.
Kent Str.

Lion Terr.
Longley St.

Female
Hosp.

Town
Hall

3

Road

Greetham S.

Belgrave S.
Russell S.

Chapel S.
Barrott S.
Hawke S.
College

St.Georges
d Ch.

St.Georges
Sq.

Park

St.Michaels
Chu.

Theatre
Royal

Hyde
Park

Grosvenor S.

Basin

Officers'
Recreation
Ground

Sunday Rd.
St.Michael's Rd.

Common

Victoria
Hall
Wiltshire

St.Vincent Rd.
West St.
Service St.
Middle St.

St.James Road

Waterloo

Men's
Recreation
Ground

Cambridge Rd.

Sackville

Durham S.

Colewort
Barracks

Warblington

Gun Wharf Rd.
St.Mary
Kings S.
Lombard S.

St.Thomas S.

General's Ho.

Cambridge
Barracks Rd.

St.Pauls
Chu.

St.Paul's Rd.
York S.

King Street

Norfolk S.

Green Rd.

TSMOUTH

Ch.
Mns.

PeacY

High
St.
Nicholas S.

Victoria
Barracks

Kings Road

SO

Pembroke

Clarence
Barracks

Officers
Qrs.
The Clarence

Handbrook
Grove Road

St.Edw.

Elm

Old
Stone Rd.

A
PORTSMOUTH
MISCELLANY

MARK BARDELL

A PORTSMOUTH MISCELLANY

Summersdale Publishers Ltd
46 West Street
Chichester
West Sussex
PO19 1RP
UK

www.summersdale.com

Printed and bound by CPI Group (UK) Ltd, Croydon, CR0 4YY

ISBN: 978-1-84953-463-5

Substantial discounts on bulk quantities of Summersdale books are available to corporations, professional associations and other organisations. For details contact Nicky Douglas by telephone: +44 (0) 1243 756902, fax: +44 (0) 1243 786300 or email: nicky@summersdale.com.

A
PORTSMOUTH MISCELLANY

PHIL HEWITT

summersdale

PORTSMOUTH

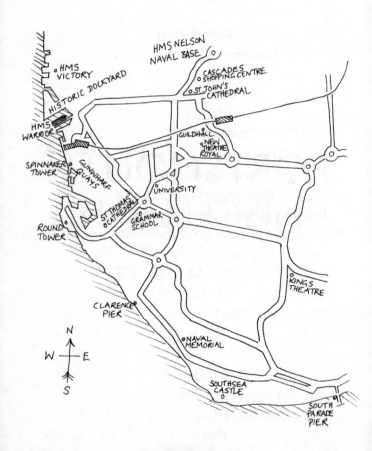

CONTENTS

Portsmouth People

Portsmouth Culture

FOREWORD

by Dillie Keane

Congratulations! You've purchased *A Portsmouth Miscellany!* Well, OK, you may just be standing in a bookshop to get out of the rain, and having idly opened this book, you're now wondering whether to buy it or not. Or perhaps you just opened it in someone else's bathroom. In which case you'll need your own copy. Whichever, however, whatever, congratulations to you, dear reader, for having the sheer good sense to open it at all because this is a feast of a book that will launch you into a seaside city which offers far more than first meets the eye.

Of course, it's entirely possible that Portsmouth exists for you only as the place where you once caught a ferry to somewhere warmer and more exotic (the Isle of Wight). You may be slightly more familiar with the city and its impressive Historic Dockyard, you may have toured the *Victory* and tripped over the plaque where Nelson also fell (silly place to put a plaque). Or you may, like me, have spent a lifetime training your bare feet to endure walking on hurty-hurty stones (ouch!) in order to swim off Southsea's long and gorgeous beach. Whichever way, this book is bound to delight, instruct and entertain.

My own connection with Portsmouth began when I first entered the world in 1952 in a nursing home in Yarborough Road. My parents had moved here from Ireland because my dad fancied practising medicine in England, and they chose it because they wanted to live near the sea. The week after they moved here, war broke out. I don't think the two events were connected, although my mother could be pretty aggressive. So my three siblings and I grew up in this crowded and boisterous city, which has not only a strong Irish community but in fact is home to communities from all over the world, thanks to its many centuries of sea connections with other nations.

But perhaps for a true Portsmouthian, the greatest distance one can leap is the 20 or so miles westwards up the road to our long-time rival, Southampton. My long-time collaborator in Fascinating Aida, Adèle Anderson, was born there, and I like to think the two of us have done our bit to bring these two great cities together harmoniously over the years. But I still hate it when Southampton FC win.

Portsmouth holds a very dear place in my heart, and I still think of it as home. I've performed too many times to mention here in the Kings Theatre, and the New Theatre Royal. In fact, my connection with the Kings goes right back to my schooldays when I volunteered myself to do *anything* – I'd have gladly swept the stage – and I spent many happy holidays working as an usher, barmaid, box office girl, and finally Assistant Stage Manager. Nowadays I'm proud to be one of this beautiful Matcham theatre's patrons.

Pompey folk don't stand on ceremony – it's a straight-talking city with open-hearted citizens – and I sometimes wonder if my no-holds-barred songwriting style found its first seeds of inspiration here. This friendly and funny city is full of fascinating places for you to discover, and Phil Hewitt's delightful book is packed with information on its sights, its culture and its huge importance throughout history that will make you want to explore for yourself. You might even decide not to take that ferry after all.

Dillie Keane
September 2013
www.fascinatingaida.co.uk

Welcome to Portsmouth

*At Portsmouth the town dweller is in touch
with a different world. Motor and train have
brought him to a corner of Hampshire, where
at every turn he is confronted by a uniform, a
scene or a monument that carries his thoughts
at a bound to the other side of the world.*
GUIDE TO SOUTHSEA AND PORTSMOUTH
(WARD, LOCK, 1947)

Not many cities tell you exactly what they are in their name alone. There's something pleasingly transparent about the very name Portsmouth – a name which tells us why it developed where it did and in the way it has. Portsmouth sits at the mouth of a port, a simple fact which has shaped the city's entire history.

And what a history it has been.

Whichever way you look at it, Portsmouth – Britain's only island city – is a city of distinction. You could argue that other cities are more beautiful, but I defy anyone to name one that is more interesting. Portsmouth is a place steeped in its own traditions, but it's also a place which likes to look at the wider horizons. Centuries of ambition and endeavour turned Portsmouth into the most significant port in Britain in the eighteenth and nineteenth centuries. At its peak, it was one of the most important in the world, its great dockyard the starting point for a navy which conquered an empire.

Take a stroll along the seafront at Southsea, and the wealth of memorials shows you Portsmouth's place in the world. Today, rather more modestly, it stands as one of Europe's busiest ferry ports.

But it is also the city which gave us Charles Dickens; the city in which Sherlock Holmes was conceived; and the city in which Isambard Kingdom Brunel first saw the light of day.

A remarkable number of writers, artists, musicians, actors and performers have been born here or lived here or died here. Great adventurers have started their days in the city; so too have great men of religion, reformers, humanitarians and politicians. Put them all together, and it is a fascinating tale they tell.

Come with me now as we take a look at **Portsmouth Times**, at **Portsmouth Places**, at **Portsmouth People** and at **Portsmouth Culture**. A captivating journey lies ahead. ⋀ modest !

Phil Hewitt
September 2013

OVERVIEW

Situated 74 miles south-west of London and 19 miles south-east of Southampton, Portsmouth is the second-largest city in Hampshire and the most densely populated city in the UK. Southampton's residential population outstrips Portsmouth's population of 207,100 (2011), but nowhere else in the country comes quite as densely packed as Portsmouth – not even London. The capital is home to around 350 fewer people per square mile than Portsmouth's 13,330 – a remarkable statistic which it is not hard to explain.

Portsmouth sits on Portsea Island, separated from the English mainland by 100 metres of water at high tide. Of course, Portsmouth has long since breached the borders of its island home. The second half of the twentieth century saw it spread relentlessly northwards across the water. But there's no doubting that Portsmouth still retains an identity which directly reflects its unique location on a small spit of land in the English Channel.

Formerly part of Hampshire County Council, Portsmouth, like Southampton, became administratively independent of Hampshire in 1997 with the creation of a unitary authority. Portsmouth City Council is solely responsible for all the city's services. The city elects forty-two councillors to fourteen wards across the authority. The city is represented by two Members of Parliament in the House of Commons, one for Portsmouth South and one for Portsmouth North.

The Origins of Portsmouth

If you are looking for the origins of Portsmouth, look no further than Portchester Castle, built by Romans in the late third century at the head of Portsmouth Harbour, then taken over by the Saxons after the Romans left Britain. The castle remains the best-preserved of the Roman Saxon Shore forts.

Meanwhile the settlement which became Portsmouth started to develop closer to the mouth of the harbour, just to the south-east on Portsea

Island. Although Portsmouth did not yet exist as a town, its favourable position as a landing place was evidently recognised.

The story runs that in AD 501 a band of Saxons, under Porth (or Port), landed with his two sons Bieda and Mægla 'at a certain place which is called Portes Mūtha' and there killed a noble young Briton – a colourful story historians are happy to dismiss.

In fact, the name speaks for itself. The Romans had probably called the place 'Portus', Latin for harbour. The word was modified in Old English, and the word 'mūtha' or 'mouth' was added. Portsmouth therefore means literally: 'Mouth of the harbour called Port'. The settlement was first recorded as Portesmuthan in the late ninth century, and eventually became Portsmouth.

By the time of the Domesday Book (1086), Portsea Island was home to three manors: Buckland, Copnor and Frodington, names still in use today although Frodington has since become Fratton.

As the *Victoria County History* says:

> *With the Norman Conquest and the*
> *consequent closer relations between England*
> *and the continent, such a harbour could not*
> *fail to become of importance.*
> A HISTORY OF THE COUNTY OF HAMPSHIRE:
> VOLUME 3 (1908)

Portsea Island, on which Portsmouth sits, separates two inlets from the English Channel; to the east is Langstone Harbour; to the west is Portsmouth Harbour, between Gosport and Portsmouth – 15 square miles of water including lakes and creeks. Protecting it all to the south is the Isle of Wight. All the elements were there: Portsmouth Harbour was the perfect place for a naval base to develop. All it now needed was Richard the Lionheart.

Richard I, king of England from 1189 to 1199, was probably the first to recognise Portsmouth's full potential, granting the town its charter in 1194 and letting out its land for development. Richard adopted the star and crescent as his symbol, and historians believe that the town of Portsmouth adopted it in turn as a tribute to him. The star and crescent remains to this day the Portsmouth coat of arms.

The Country's Chief Naval Base

To write the history of Portsmouth in the 18th century would involve writing the history of the British Navy and the most glorious period of its annals.

CHARPENTIER'S GUIDE TO PORTSMOUTH AND SOUTHSEA (1913)

Following on from the work laid down by King Richard, the docks were of sufficient importance by the reign of King John (1199–1216) to warrant special protection. On 20 May 1212 by royal order, John effectively founded the Royal Dockyard:

The King to the Sheriff of Southampton &c. We order you, without delay, by the view of lawful men, to cause our docks at Portsmouth to be inclosed with a good and strong wall,

in such a manner as our beloved and faithful
William archdeacon of Taunton will tell you,
for the preservation of our ships and galleys;
and likewise to cause penthouses to be made
to the same walls, as the same archdeacon
will also tell you, in which all our ships' tackle
may be safely kept: and use as much dispatch
as you can, in order that the same may be
completed this summer, lest in the ensuing
winter our ships and galleys and their rigging
should incur any damage by your default.
And when we know the cost, it shall be
accounted to you.
CLOSE ROLLS OF KING JOHN (1212)

The Forest of Bere and the New Forest were ready sources of timber, a fact which almost certainly helped dictate the location, but after King John's declaration, progress was slow for the next two and a half centuries. It wasn't until the late 1400s that things moved on significantly, when Henry VII (reigned 1485–1509) placed the Royal Navy and Portsmouth Dockyard on a more solid and efficient footing. In doing so, he brought new life to a town which had been in the doldrums. With the building of new docks, employment rose, brew houses were built, languishing trades started to flourish, new trades were introduced and exports began to rise.

In 1495 Henry VII gave Portsmouth its first dry dock, today the world's oldest surviving dry dock still in use. Henry VIII (reigned 1509–1547) continued his father's work. Convinced of its importance, Henry VIII invested large sums of money in the Dockyard. Growth faltered again in the second half of the sixteenth century before picking up and accelerating in the eighteenth and nineteenth centuries. During the reign of Henry VIII, the Dockyard covered eight acres; by the outbreak of the First World War, it covered 300 acres.

By the time of the reign of Charles II (1660–1685), Portsmouth was the country's chief naval base. The present wall around the Dockyard was started in 1704 and completed in 1711, the start of a century which confirmed Portsmouth's national importance. In 1729 a Naval College was opened in the Dockyard for the education of young naval officers. The eighteenth century saw no fewer than 66 ships of war launched at Portsmouth. In the nineteenth century, a remarkable 148 vessels were built in Portsmouth Dockyard. Further significant extension to the Dockyard began in 1864.

A century ago, Portsmouth considered itself 'the world's greatest naval port' – a claim made by the writers of the *Southsea and Portsmouth Coronation Souvenir Guide*, which was issued free by the Southsea and Portsmouth Entertainment Committee in June 1911 to mark the coronation of King George V on 22 June. The evidence of the previous couple of centuries amply justified the label the city so grandly gave itself. By the early 1920s the British Empire covered almost a quarter of the earth's total land area and comprised around 458 million people. Portsmouth had been its launch pad.

Ironically perhaps, given that France was the reason for much of Portsmouth's naval activity, the opening scenes of the film version of the musical *Les Misérables* were filmed in Portsmouth Dockyard. Based on Victor Hugo's great nineteenth-century novel, the film – released in January 2013 – opens with Hugh Jackman as the convict Jean Valjean helping to haul a ship into dry dock under the stern gaze of the dogged Inspector Javert (Russell Crowe).

Naval life, rarely if ever plain sailing, spilled over into outright mutiny off Portsmouth in 1797, when sailors on sixteen ships in the Channel Fleet at Spithead effectively immobilised themselves at a time when the country was at war with revolutionary France. The Admiralty's apparent disregard for the sailors who served was the trigger. Pay, conditions and leave were the men's grievances in a strike which lasted from 16 April to 15 May. **Admiral Lord Howe** (1726–1799) emerged as the key figure in bringing it all to an end, negotiating a settlement which involved a royal pardon for all the crews concerned and sufficient concessions to placate the sailors.

Fortifying the Town

Portsmouth's early years in the twelfth century were filled with war and preparations for war, but these were years which also saw it emerge as an important trading centre. Troops were conveyed from Portsmouth, but so too were large quantities of wheat, mostly to France and Spain. The wool trade also developed strongly in the new town. Heading in the opposite direction, wine, woad, wax and iron were among the principal imports for which Portsmouth was the port of entry.

With Portsmouth's growing importance, so too grew the need to fortify. A grim moment in 1338 saw the town heavily damaged by marauding Frenchmen. The townspeople drove the invaders back across what is now Southsea Common, but Portsmouth had paid a high price for its want of effective defences. It was virtually destroyed.

In 1415, Henry V carried out the first fleet review at Spithead before sailing to war against the French. Fortifying Portsmouth became vital, and he ordered the construction of the **Round Tower** in 1418. Built in wood, it was completed in 1426, and the **Square Tower** nearby was added in 1494, the year before the Dockyard was established.

Henry VII ordered the Round Tower to be rebuilt in stone, strengthening the fortifications considerably. A Tudor account describing 'the este side of Portesmuth Haven' notes:

> *... there is at this Point of the Haven*
> *Portesmuth Toun, and a great round Tourre*
> *almost doble in quantite and strenkith to that*
> *that is on the West side of the Haven right*
> *agayn it: and heere is a might[y] chaine of*
> *Yren to draw from Tourre to Towrre.*
> THE ITINERARY OF JOHN LELAND (1539–1543)

Southsea Castle, from which a horror-stricken Henry VIII watched the sinking of the *Mary Rose*, was built in haste in 1544 at the southernmost tip of Portsea Island, the key vantage point at the mouth of Portsmouth Harbour. Set within a strong high wall partly surrounded by a deep fosse and flanked by two batteries, it served as another defence against the ever-looming threat of invasion. Portsmouth was crucial – and Southsea Castle was part of the plan to guard it. Ramparts, defensive walls and various other fortifications were also part of the plan which gathered pace under Elizabeth I (1558–1603).

With the construction of these fortifications, the sixteenth century effectively established Portsmouth as a major town, though not necessarily a wholly prosperous one. Tudor Portsmouth was fairly squalid by most accounts.

In the early seventeenth century, Southsea Castle fell into disrepair and was damaged by fire, but renewed threat of invasion prompted Charles II to repair and improve it. The castle, still with its guns ready for action, was used as a military prison in the nineteenth century. It was bought by Portsmouth City Council in 1960, restored to its nineteenth-century appearance and opened to the public in 1967.

In the nineteenth century, the ramparts had been levelled, some of the gates taken down and the moats filled in. Early twentieth-century guides reflect the change to a more peaceful footing:

> *In accompanying our visitor on a ramble through Old Portsmouth, we may mention by the way that until comparatively recently the town was shut in by ramparts and zealously-guarded gates.*
>
> CHARPENTIER'S GUIDE TO PORTSMOUTH AND SOUTHSEA (1913)

PORTSMOUTH PEOPLE

Naval and Military Men and Women of Note

George Legge, first Baron Dartmouth (1648–1691) was clearly a man of principle, a governor of Portsmouth who died in the Tower of London in the hottest of political waters. When James II (reigned 1685–1688) fled to France, Dartmouth pledged his allegiance to William and Mary. His reward, however, was to be arrested for treason, charged with offering to give Portsmouth to the French, an accusation he strongly denied. Sadly for Dartmouth, his death in the Tower left his innocence – or indeed his guilt – unproven.

Sudden impulses are wonderful things; few have led to a story as extraordinary as that of **Mary Lacy** (*b.* 1740), the Kent woman who stole a set of men's clothes on a whim and went to sea as William Chandler. In May 1759 Mary sailed as a ship's boy, servant to the ship's carpenter. A year later, she was confined to the Royal Naval Hospital at Haslar, near Portsmouth, with pneumonia. By the time she was released, her ship had gone, so she joined the *Royal Sovereign* in Portsmouth instead on a seven-year carpenter's apprenticeship. Rumours that she was in fact a woman were swiftly dismissed by the men she worked with. A couple of years later she was to be found working at Portsmouth Dockyard where she was briefly engaged to a housemaid named Sarah Chase. Mary completed her apprenticeship, but left the service when her rheumatism worsened. Abandoning her pretence to be a man, she successfully applied to the navy for a pension under her real name. By now living in London, she married a sailor and recorded her story in 1773 as *The History of the Female Shipwright*. The book was initially successful but was rapidly forgotten, at which point Mary also disappeared from history.

Admiral Augustus Keppel (first Viscount Keppel, 1725–1786) fought in the War of the Austrian Succession, the Seven Years' War and the War of American Independence. His flagship was HMS *Victory*. However, his career was marred by the fact that he was twice court-martialled. In 1747 Keppel ran his ship the *Maidstone* ashore while chasing a French vessel. At the resulting trial, Keppel was honourably acquitted. However, he was in deep water again towards the end of his career for his actions after the First Battle of Ushant on 27 July 1778. Keppel was charged with misconduct and neglect of duty, charges which would have brought the death penalty on conviction. He was court-martialled in Portsmouth, and once again, he was acquitted. Keppel is commemorated today in the city in which he was vindicated, in the name of the Keppel's Head Hotel which opened in 1779, one of seventeen inns which stood on The Hard in the eighteenth century.

Posterity has been rather more interested in his sister Jane, but the naval officer **Sir Francis William Austen** (1774–1865) certainly wasn't without distinction. Francis excelled at the Royal Naval

Academy at Portsmouth, and in May 1799 he was promoted to captain when he captured a French brig of war attempting to break the British blockade of Napoleon's army in Egypt. He became a full admiral in 1848 and died at his home, Portsdown Lodge, Portsmouth, seventeen years later.

Sir Charles James Napier (1782–1853), the British general who conquered the province of Sind (now in Pakistan) and served as its governor from 1843 to 1847, died in Portsmouth. The unlikely story goes that he announced his triumph punningly with a little bit of Latin: 'Peccavi' ('I have sinned' – i.e. 'I have Sind'). The tale was probably hatched by the humorous magazine *Punch*.

A remarkable list of distinctions is detailed on the statue in Portsmouth Dockyard of **Bruce Austin Fraser** (1888–1981), Baron Fraser of North Cape, Admiral of the Fleet.

Fraser was Controller of the Navy from 1939 to 1942, Commander-in-Chief Home Fleet from 1943 to 1944, Commander-in-Chief Eastern Fleet 1944, Commander-in-Chief British Pacific Fleet from 1944 to 1946, Commander-in-Chief Portsmouth from 1947 to 1948 and First Sea Lord from 1948 to 1951. On 26 December 1943, Fraser commanded the British naval force that sank the German battleship *Scharnhorst* off Norway's North Cape.

Naval officer **Sir Ian Stewart McIntosh** (1919–2003) was adrift for 23 days in the Atlantic when the troopship *Britannia*, on which he was travelling, was sunk by German fire on 25 March 1941. There were eighty-two people in the overcrowded lifeboat, and McIntosh emerged a natural leader. McIntosh and third officer Bill McVicar navigated by the sun and the stars as they sailed and drifted without oars for 1,500 miles. Remarkably, they reached a point on the Brazilian coast just a few miles from the point they were targeting. There was little food, and by the time they reached land, just thirty-six of the eighty-two survived. McIntosh later said he was sustained by two things: the journey of Captain William Bligh after the *Bounty* mutiny and the memory of a Norwegian girl he had met in his native Australia. They married two years later. Vice-Admiral McIntosh died at the Queen Alexandra Hospital, Portsmouth, and was buried at St Anne's Hill cemetery in Gosport.

Three Magnificent Ships

Today the former Dockyard at Portsmouth is officially Her Majesty's Naval Base (HMNB) Portsmouth, one of three operating bases for the Royal Navy, alongside HMNB Clyde and HMNB Devonport. It is the base port for two-thirds of the Royal Navy's surface fleet.

More importantly for the general public, a large part of the site is open to visitors. Portsmouth Historic Dockyard is home to an unrivalled display of attractions, most notably three of the world's most famous warships: *Mary Rose*, HMS *Victory* and HMS *Warrior*.

A fascinating piece of naval heritage, the *Mary Rose* is once again the pride of Portsmouth after being rescued from more than four centuries at the bottom of the sea – a reminder of the ghastly day Henry VIII watched helplessly as his magnificent flagship sank off Southsea Castle on 19 July 1545. Some commentators believe the *Mary Rose* turned too quickly and submerged her open gun ports, while others contend that tidal forces and poor design were the key factors. It seems likely that large numbers of soldiers in full armour on her upper decks destabilised her further – and so she sank.

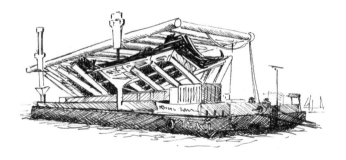

The *Mary Rose* was rediscovered in 1836 when a fishing net caught on the wreck, but she was soon forgotten again. The first serious modern search was launched in 1965; the wreck of the *Mary Rose* was rediscovered in 1971; and she was raised in 1982. The surviving section of the ship has found its permanent home in a purpose-built structure in Portsmouth Historic Dockyard. The new Mary Rose Museum opened to the public on 31 May 2013.

The Spinnaker Tower has emerged in recent years as a symbol of modern Portsmouth, but in reality it will never come close to the icon status enjoyed by Nelson's flagship at the Battle of Trafalgar, HMS *Victory*. The British Navy's fifth warship to bear the name, HMS *Victory* is the only surviving warship to have fought in the American War of Independence, the French Revolutionary War and the Napoleonic Wars – and for generations of visitors, it has proved one of the city's most powerful magnets.

HMS *Victory* was built in Chatham Dockyard in Kent and launched on 7 May 1765 as a first-rate ship of the line, weighing 2,162 tons and mounting 100 guns. Her overall length was 69 metres and her beam 16 metres. She had a crew of more than 800 men. Her first commission was as flagship of Admiral Augustus Keppel (1725–1786), and from 1798 to 1800 she served as a hospital ship for the prison hulks before undergoing an extensive refit.

Before the Battle of Trafalgar on Monday, 21 October 1805, the *Victory*'s flags gave Nelson's famous signal, 'England expects that every man will do his duty', and every man duly did. Nelson was standing on the deck of the *Victory* when he was shot and fatally wounded. By the time Nelson died, just over three hours later, a great victory had been won.

HMS *Victory*'s active career ended seven years later in 1812 when she was moored off Gosport in Portsmouth Harbour and used as a depot ship. The town of Gosport contributed £75 a year towards the *Victory*'s maintenance. For a while, HMS *Victory* served as the Naval School of Telegraphy, but her condition was deteriorating significantly. The Society for Nautical Research led a national appeal, and on 12 January 1922 the *Victory* was taken into dry dock in the Dockyard where work began to restore her to her condition at the time of the Battle of Trafalgar. Excitement began to mount as the unveiling neared, perfectly captured in the 1928 official Portsmouth guide:

> *She was built by the nation, she fought for the nation, and she has been saved by the money of the nation as a lasting memorial for all time of England's greatness.*
>
> THE OFFICIAL GUIDE TO SOUTHSEA, PUBLISHED BY THE PORTSMOUTH CORPORATION, 1928.

Unlike the *Mary Rose* and HMS *Victory*, HMS *Warrior*, the most recent of Portsmouth's great trio of warships, is still afloat, moored at her purpose-built jetty just outside the Historic Dockyard – a proud reminder of Britain's nineteenth-century naval pre-eminence.

The first ironclad ship built for the British Navy, HMS *Warrior* was the largest warship in the world, intended as a riposte to the French armoured ship *La Gloire*. In building HMS *Warrior*, the British were determined to make a point: the French really shouldn't take on the Royal Navy. Her sheer size

remains deeply impressive, and today, across four vast decks, the visitor gains a fascinating insight into what life must have been like for a Victorian sailor on board a nineteenth-century warship.

Powered by steam as well as sail, HMS *Warrior* is the only surviving member of Queen Victoria's Black Battle Fleet. Designed by Isaac Watts, the Royal Navy's chief constructor, she was launched at Blackwall on the River Thames in 1860, measuring 127.4 metres in length and with a beam of 17.6 metres. Weighing 9,210 tons, HMS *Warrior* carried 705 officers and men and was armed with twenty-six 68-pounder muzzle loaders and ten 110-pounder and four 40-pounder breech loaders. Renamed *Vernon III* in 1904, she became part of the Vernon torpedo school at Portsmouth until she was removed from the Navy List in 1923, after which she served as an oil fuel pier at Pembroke for fifty years. She was towed to Hartlepool, restored to her former glory by the Warrior Preservation Trust at a cost of £7 million and returned to Portsmouth in June 1987 as a major visitor attraction.

The sinking of the *Mary Rose* off Portsmouth was not the port's only great tragedy. The loss of the HMS *Royal George* more than two centuries later ranks as one of the worst maritime disasters in British waters. Estimates range widely as to the number of men to perish. The general agreement is at least 800, perhaps as many as 1,200.

A 100-gun first-rate ship of the line of the Royal Navy, HMS *Royal George* was the largest warship in the world when she was launched in 1756. She survived the Seven Years' War but did not survive routine maintenance work off Portsmouth on 29 August 1782. Rotting timbers are the most likely cause of the sinking. A large number of workmen were aboard, plus several hundred wives and relatives visiting the sailors. Also swelling the casualty numbers were various traders selling their wares.

PORTSMOUTH PLACES

Portsmouth, a Two-Cathedral City

The understated beauty of Portsmouth Cathedral inspires the many visitors that come here. Its light coloured stone and towering bronze doors change their hue with the seasons and with the rising and setting of the sun.

PORTSMOUTH CATHEDRAL WEBSITE

The **Cathedral Church of St Thomas of Canterbury**, situated off the High Street in Old Portsmouth, is one of the country's newer cathedrals, but it certainly isn't one of the city's newer buildings. Formerly Portsmouth Parish Church, the church dates from about 1180 when Jean de Gisors, a wealthy Norman merchant and Lord of the Manor of Titchfield, gave land in the town of Portsmouth to the Augustinian canons of Southwick Priory in order to build a chapel 'to the glorious honour of the martyr Thomas of Canterbury, one time Archbishop'. However, only the chancel, chancel aisles and transepts of the original church remain. Together, they are considered among the finest examples in Hampshire of the transition period of early English architecture – sadly a distinction which did not save the building from severe damage during the English Civil War in 1642, after which much of the church had to be rebuilt. A new tower was added at the western front in 1691. Much of the rest dates from 1693 to 1718.

St Thomas' became the mother church of the new diocese of Portsmouth in 1927, one of a number of dioceses created in the first third of the twentieth century. Birmingham (1905), Southwark (1905), Chelmsford (1914), Bury St Edmunds (1914), Coventry (1918) and Bradford (1920) were the first, followed by Derby, Guildford, Leicester and Portsmouth seven years later. The new diocese of Portsmouth was carved out of the old diocese of Winchester.

Various changes were made to fit the church to serve as a cathedral, including the addition of a throne for the new bishop.

The **Cathedral Church of St John the Evangelist**, built in the French Gothic architectural style, is the Roman Catholic Cathedral of Portsmouth. Constructed from red Fareham brick and Portland stone on Bishop Crispian Way, just west of the city centre, it is the seat of the Roman Catholic Bishop of Portsmouth and also the mother church of the Catholic diocese of Portsmouth.

At the beginning of the eighteenth century, Portsmouth's Catholic community numbered barely more than a hundred, but in the early years of the nineteenth century, the numbers swelled significantly. A Catholic chapel, built in Portsea in

1796, proved too small for their needs and was twice extended, but large numbers of Catholic soldiers in the Portsmouth garrison meant that a more radical solution was needed. Land became available when the redundant defensive ramparts around Portsea were demolished, and it was bought in 1877 to be the site of a larger church. John Crawley designed the new building, but did not live to see it completed and was succeeded by Stanislaus Hansom.

The new diocese of Portsmouth, formerly part of the diocese of Southwark, was created in May 1882 by Pope Leo XII, and the new cathedral was opened three months later, with John Vertue as its first bishop. The building lost all but one of its original stained-glass windows during the Second World War when the bishop's house next door was destroyed, but restoration works were carried out in the 1950s and the cathedral continues to thrive. In 2010, a statue of St John the Evangelist, the work of internationally acclaimed Midhurst-based sculptor Philip Jackson, was unveiled outside.

PORTSMOUTH PEOPLE

Portsmouth's Adventurers

Given Portsmouth's place in the world, it comes as no surprise that the city has long been associated with adventurers and explorers with their sights set on the far horizons.

Admiral Arthur Phillip (1738–1814) has gone down in history as the first Governor of New South Wales and the founder of the settlement which became Sydney. With Phillip as captain-general of the expedition, the fleet set sail from Portsmouth on 13 May 1787, reaching Botany Bay on 18 January 1788. Rejecting it, he moved on to a more favourable place which he named Sydney Cove. He landed there on 26 January 1788, a date now celebrated as Australia Day.

Polynesian islander **Omai** (*c.*1751–*c.*1780) first set foot on British soil in Portsmouth on 14 July 1774 to be greeted by Lord Sandwich, First Lord of the Admiralty. The idea was to introduce him in London as a 'noble savage', an example of the kind of humanity the celebrated Captain Cook and his comrades were discovering on their travels. It is said that when he was presented to George III at Kew, Omai remarked: 'How do, King Tosh!' Other treats on his visit included trips to the theatre, the races and game-shooting on the North Yorkshire Moors. Omai returned home with Cook in 1776, bearing all sorts of British goodies. Quite what he thought of Portsmouth is not recorded.

Polar explorer **William Lashly** was born on 25 December 1867 at Hambledon, 12 miles north of Portsmouth, the city in which he died on 12 June 1940 at the Royal Hospital. Lashly volunteered to serve on Captain Robert Falcon Scott's British

National Antarctic Expedition (1901–04) and clearly impressed. When Scott began recruiting for the Terra Nova expedition of 1910, with the South Pole as his goal, he chose Lashly among the men he wanted with him. Lashly served as second engineer. Ultimately, it was Lashly's sad fate to form part of the search party that found Scott's body on 12 November 1912.

Serving with Lashly was **Edgar Evans** (1876–1912). Evans joined the Royal Navy at the age of fifteen and, after training at Falmouth, served as a physical training instructor in Portsmouth. Evans was sought out by Scott for the National Antarctic Expedition of 1901–1904, after which he returned to Portsmouth where he qualified as a gunnery instructor, married and had two children. In 1910 he joined Scott's second Antarctic expedition. Evans served as sledgemaster in charge of rigging and repairs, but sadly the expedition was to end in well-documented tragedy. A big man, he apparently suffered worse than the others from tiredness and the food shortages. Several falls left him in a poor state, and he died on 17 February 1912, unfairly gaining the reputation that he was the first to crack and effectively hampered the others. Kinder interpretations focus on the isolation he suffered as a rating among officers. He was posthumously awarded the Polar Medal.

Charles Montagu Doughty's monumental two-volume *Travels in Arabia Deserta* (1888) remains his lasting legacy. One of the most important British explorers of Arabia, Doughty (1843–1926) was also a travel writer and poet. Born in Suffolk, he was educated at the Beach House School, Portsmouth. Originally intending a career in the Royal Navy, he developed instead an interest in geology and archaeology, followed by travels in the 1870s to Nazareth, Jerusalem, Bethlehem, Hebron and Damascus. He ended up wandering in Arabia for almost two years.

William Shakespear – no, not that one, but William Henry Irvine Shakespear (1878–1915), the diplomat and explorer who mapped uncharted areas of Northern Arabia – was born in what is now Pakistan and educated at Portsmouth Grammar School (1889–1893). He goes down in history as the first British official to make contact with Ibn Sa'ud, the future king of the modern state of Saudi Arabia which Ibn Sa'ud founded in 1932. Shakespear tried to persuade his British paymasters to take Ibn Sa'ud more seriously; Ibn Sa'ud was keen for British protection and British recognition. Sadly, death on the battlefield was Shakespear's fate. Ibn Sa'ud had urged Shakespear to retreat, but he was killed by a stray bullet when Ibn Sa'ud's men fought their traditional enemies, the Al Rashid, at the Battle of Jarrab.

William Launcelot Scott Fleming (1906–1990) managed to be a bishop, an explorer and a geologist. Specialising in geology at Cambridge and ordained as a priest, he combined the two when he joined the British Graham Land expedition to Antarctica (1934–1937) as chaplain and geologist. On his return, he contributed to the *Geographical Journal*'s account of the expedition. After serving during the Second World War as a chaplain in the Royal Naval Volunteer Reserve, he was appointed director of the Scott Polar Research Institute in 1947. He became Bishop of Portsmouth in 1949 and Bishop of Norwich in 1959.

Plenty of us still remember packing the beaches in eager anticipation of the safe return to Portsmouth of round-the-world yachtsman **Sir Alec Rose** (1908–1991) on board his *Lively Lady*. Rose first went to sea during the Second World War after joining the Royal Naval Volunteer Reserve, but was invalided out in 1945. By the early 1960s he and his wife Dorothy were running a greengrocer's shop in Southsea. However, the sea still loomed large for Rose, and recreational sailing became an increasingly important part of his life. His crowning adventure was to circumnavigate the globe single-handedly in 1967–1968. As the *Oxford Dictionary of National Biography* notes: 'He was not the first, nor the fastest, but his feat, by an ordinary man in an elderly boat, captured the public imagination.' Unsponsored, he paid for everything himself when he set out on 16 July 1967. Three-hundred-and-fifty-four days and 28,500 miles later, crowds more than a quarter of a million strong gathered to see him land at Portsmouth where his reward was a knighthood.

Glaciologist and polar explorer **Roy Martindale Koerner** took part in an expedition which Prime Minister Harold Wilson described at the time as 'a feat of endurance and courage which ranks with any in polar history'. Koerner (1932–2008) was born at 40 Kimbolton Road, Portsmouth and attended Portsmouth Southern Grammar School and Sheffield University. From 1967 to 1969 he was a member of the four-man British Trans-Arctic Expedition led by Walter Herbert. They reached the North Pole on 5 April 1969 after covering 3,620 miles, the first surface crossing of the Arctic Ocean. It was only the second expedition to reach the North Pole.

Portsmouth During the English Civil War

During the English Civil War, Portsmouth was an obvious target for the Parliamentarians who made it their policy to secure for themselves the chief maritime towns. Before the First Civil War (1642–1646), in the interests of strengthening Portsmouth, **Colonel George Goring**, its governor, was guilty of double-dealing, taking money from both sides. But his declaration for the king on 2 August 1642 was a significant one, opening up the possibility of the beleaguered Charles I receiving relief from the continent through the gateway of a supposedly sympathetic Portsmouth. Goring promptly found himself under siege. The king's ships effectively switched sides. Declaring for Parliament, they prevented stores from being brought in. Early in September the guns from Parliamentarian Gosport opened fire on Portsmouth. Southsea Castle surrendered, and with no help coming from the king, many of the soldiers in the town saw resistance as pointless. Their officers were forced to surrender on 4 September.

Sir William Waller (*c.*1598–1668) was the victorious Parliamentary commander who then went on to take several other south-coast towns and cities, including Chichester. His efforts won him the nickname 'William the Conqueror'. Waller was among the first to argue in favour of a professional army which came into being as the New Model Army in February 1645. Goring meanwhile had reached the Netherlands, where he helped raise money and men for the royalist cause and proved a particular thorn in the Parliamentarian side in the Second Civil War (1648–49).

Louise-Renée de Kéroualle, Duchess of Portsmouth, Countess of Fareham, Baroness Petersfield (1649–1734) lived and died in France, but in between times, she was the mistress of Charles II of Great Britain, who bestowed her English titles on her in 1673. Their son, Charles Lennox (1672–1723), became the first Duke of Richmond. Charles Lennox died at Goodwood, just east of Chichester, seat of the Dukes of Richmond ever since.

Eighteenth-Century and Regency Writers

Numerous writers down the centuries have enjoyed associations – happy or otherwise – with the city of Portsmouth.

Sadly, Portsmouth came as a monumental disappointment to the travelling African **Ukawsaw Gronniosaw** (also known as **James Albert**), who lived in England and recorded his impressions under the not particularly natty title *Most Remarkable Particulars in the Life of James Albert Ukawsaw Gronniosaw, an African Prince, as Related by Himself* (1772). Gronniosaw was born of royal descent in Nigeria in about 1705 and regarded it as a dream fulfilled when he arrived in England in 1762. However, Portsmouth did not prove the best introduction. He was cheated of his money and appalled by what he saw as crudity and dishonesty all around him. He declared England to be 'worse than Sodom'. He moved to London where he fared rather better, but disappears from history after the publication of his memoir.

Susanna Rowson, née Haswell, (*c.*1762–1824) was a novelist, poet, playwright, religious writer, stage actress and educator. She was baptised at St Thomas' Parish Church, now Portsmouth Cathedral, and it was in Portsmouth that she spent her first few years until her father, a Royal navy lieutenant, took her to Massachusetts where his job was to collect revenue for the navy. The family were imprisoned during the American War of Independence and returned to England in 1778. Eight years later, Susanna published her first novel, *Victoria*. After her marriage to William Rowson, she embarked on a career as an actress, while continuing to write. The couple moved to Boston, Massachusetts, where Susanna opened her Young Ladies' Academy. She went on to write a number of textbooks, mostly on geography and history. Her novel *Charlotte: a Tale of Truth* (1791) proved particularly popular in the States.

After being transported for theft, **James Hardy Vaux** (*b.* 1782) managed to wangle his way home to England, arriving in Portsmouth. However, he was convicted of theft once again and was returned to Sydney – sufficient adventure to prompt him to write his life story, *Memoirs of James Hardy Vaux*, which was published in 1819. This time he made his way back to Ireland where he dabbled in forged bank notes and was transported for a third time, arriving in Australia once again in May 1831.

Fragments from Remarks of Twenty-Five Years in every Quarter of the Globe on Electricity, Magnetism, Aerolites, and Various Other Phenomena Of Nature probably isn't the world's best book title, but it summed up many of the achievements of **William Pringle Green** (1785–1846), a naval officer and mechanical engineer who was born in Nova Scotia and came to Portsmouth as a lieutenant in 1842. Ever ingenious, he devoted his career to dreaming up inventions to improve navy life, many of which were adopted. Rigging and lifting and lowering equipment were among his innovations. He died in Portsmouth in 1846, leaving a widow and ten children. !

PORTSMOUTH PLACES

Portsea

From the sixteenth century until the middle of the nineteenth century, Portsmouth was effectively a garrison town, with large numbers of soldiers crammed into the already overcrowded Portsea Island, leading to a decline in living conditions. The town was infested with smugglers and pirates; poverty was widespread; and illness – particularly smallpox and the plague during the seventeenth century – was rife.

Towards the end of the eighteenth century, the growth of the town of **Portsea**, alongside the Dockyard gates on the western side of Portsea Island, brought much-needed relief to the overfull older parts of the town. It developed principally to house the Dockyard workers on a site previously known as Portsmouth Common, taking the name Portsea in 1792. The *Victoria County History* gives a striking impression of what it was like just over a century later.

The streets are narrow, and the houses for the most part low, with tiled roofs and doors approached by two steps from the street. Some of the lowest houses are still known as 'garrison houses,' because, it is said, the inhabitants were not allowed to build them higher lest they should interfere with the outlook from the old fortifications. Still narrower, ill-paved alleys intersect the town in its poorest parts. The high walls of the dockyard bound it on two sides, while along the third runs the Hard, a roadway leading by the harbour-side to the main gates of the yard.

A HISTORY OF THE COUNTY OF HAMPSHIRE: VOLUME 3 (1908)

Portsea was the product of a period of great growth. The eighteenth century saw new barracks erected and the garrison strengthened. War – or the threat of it – meant good business for both town and

Dockyard. The city gained a string of new churches: the High Street Chapel, St Ann's in the Dockyard, St George's and St John's, Portsea. Population was clearly climbing, and continued to grow rapidly in the eighteenth and nineteenth centuries, particularly with the American and Napoleonic Wars, but with that growth, the town's social ills worsened.

Philanthropists and Humanitarians

Portsmouth's privations inevitably inspired a host of humanitarians determined to make their city, and indeed their country, a better place to live.

Penitent prostitutes, foundlings and those suffering the 'pernicious' effects of drinking tea were among the vast array of causes espoused by the celebrated, if rather controversial, Portsmouth-born philanthropist **Jonas Hanway** (1712–1786).

In his early years, Hanway travelled widely before turning his attention to others, setting up the Marine Society in 1756 to encourage boys into naval careers. He also campaigned in favour of Sunday schools, espoused the cause of chimney sweeps' child apprentices and set up a new hospital for the treatment of venereal disease. His writings include *Thoughts on the Duty of a Good Citizen, with Regard to War and Invasion* (1756) and *Virtue in Humble Life* (1774). One of his stranger distinctions was that he was the first man to carry an umbrella in the streets of London.

There was hardly a cause he didn't support, some distinctly more questionable than others. Hanway was guilty of a marked anti-Semitism, strongly opposing the naturalisation of Jews in Britain, claiming it would harm British interests both at home and abroad. Inevitably, he was a figure who divided opinion. Thomas Carlyle labelled him a 'dull, worthy man', and Samuel Johnson observed that Hanway had 'acquired some reputation by travelling abroad, but lost it all by travelling at home.'

John Pounds (1766–1839) was a man fond of birds – so fond in fact that he often expressed a wish that he might drop off his perch in the same unconsidered fashion. It was a suitably humble hope for a man whose primary concern was always for others: 'a poor insignificant cobbler, whose heart overflowed with desires for the betterment not of himself but of the poverty-stricken children around him' (*Guide to Southsea and Portsmouth*, 1947). Pounds' extraordinary achievement was that he translated those desires into something which genuinely made a difference. His aims were always 'to chase away ignorance, to relieve distress, and to teach the Gospel.'

Born in St Mary Street, Portsmouth, Pounds was apprenticed at the age of twelve to a shipwright, but when he fell into a dry dock in 1781, he was left permanently disabled. Pounds returned to St Mary Street to become a shoe-mender, but soon he turned his workshop into a centre of learning. Scouring the streets for poor and homeless children, he would teach them the essentials of reading and writing.

Pounds' school for the free education of destitute children was not the first, but he was certainly among the earliest, accepting only the poorest and the most ragged children he could find. He fed and cared for them, and gave them practical knowledge which gave them hope. Hundreds of street children passed through his doors during the 1820s and until his death in 1839. Five years later, in 1844, the creation of the Ragged Schools Union put the movement on a national footing. More than a quarter of a million youngsters passed through London's Ragged Schools in the middle years of the century, and soon most large towns had ragged schools.

Portsmouth would like to think that its celebrated 'crippled cobbler' was an example for much that followed. The town honoured him by establishing a number of ragged schools in his name. Charles Dickens may well have provided his own special tribute; his portrayal of the schoolmaster in *The Old Curiosity Shop* (1841) may have been inspired by Pounds.

Forton Road in Gosport was an unlikely starting place in life for a champion of Italian unity. **Jessie Jane Meriton White Mario** (1832–1906) was the daughter of a shipwright who fostered in her an interest in European democracy, particularly in Mazzini's Young Italy movement. She was introduced to Mazzini who asked her to undertake a lecture tour of British cities, and she married Mazzini's associate Alberto Mario in Portsmouth in 1857. In 1860 they joined the Sicilian campaign waged by Garibaldi, one of the founding fathers of the Italian state. Jessie worked as a nurse, eventually becoming Garibaldi's chief of ambulances. The Marios remained in Italy after unification. A selection of her papers was published posthumously in 1909 as *The Birth of Modern Italy*.

Sarah Robinson (1834–1921) was a remarkable woman who battled prejudice, indifference and her own poor health to found Portsmouth's Soldiers' Institute. An evangelist and army temperance activist, she became fascinated by all things military early in her life and determined to work with the army's roughs and toughs to improve their lot.

Realising that drunkenness was a particular problem among the lower ranks, Robinson travelled around the country, promoting prayer, distributing the Bible and offering soldiers non-alcoholic drink and cheap food. She also campaigned to improve soldiers' education, entertainment and accommodation, winning the title 'the Soldier's Friend'.

Among her most celebrated achievements was setting up the Portsmouth Soldiers' Institute in 1874, raising the money to convert The Fountain inn in Portsmouth High Street into a place of safe

Christian accommodation for soldiers in need. Some of the locals weren't too impressed with her repeated description of Portsmouth as 'Satan's very seat', but she soldiered on despite strong opposition, winning through to see her Portsmouth efforts widely admired as a model of their kind.

Born in Portsmouth, the novelist and philanthropist **Sir Walter Besant** (1836–1901) made his name as a friend to London's poor. His 1882 novel *All Sorts and Conditions of Men* reflected his impressions of the East London slums. Besant wrote with a purpose when he wrote about London's social evils: he wanted to raise awareness, and he did so. Consequently conditions improved. Besant espoused the cause of exploited workers in the sweatshops in London's East End and was instrumental in the creation of the People's Palace on the Mile End Road, a centre devoted to working-class recreation. Besant ran its literary club, as well as campaigning for free public libraries.

A mother figure to the nation's seafarers, **Dame Agnes Elizabeth Weston** (1840–1918) is one of Portsmouth's most celebrated humanitarians, a philanthropist and temperance activist who made her mark on Victorian England. Born in London, Weston was an evangelical Anglican determined to improve the lives of the men who went to sea – partly by steering them away from alcohol. Weston's monthly newsletters were circulated to every ship in the fleet, but her greatest achievements were on dry land with the setting up of overnight accommodation known as the Sailors' Rests, later Royal Sailors' Rests, for which she raised large amounts of money. Plymouth opened in 1876 and Portsmouth in 1881 on sites close to the dockyards. The rests were affectionately known as Aggie Weston's, and appropriately, they became her home. She worked tirelessly for the seafarers, but also supported their wives and children. She was criticised for the way she depicted sailors as drunken and irresponsible, but there was no doubt that she made a significant difference to thousands of sailors in need.

At some stage every Oxford student will have pushed back the frontiers of knowledge in the Bodleian Library, named after its benefactor **Sir Thomas Bodley** (1545–1613). Bodley was educated at Magdalen College, Oxford, and elected a fellow of Merton College where he is buried. In 1584 he was returned to Parliament for Portsmouth. He didn't remain its representative for long. At the next Parliament, he became the member for St Germans in Cornwall. There, as in Portsmouth, it seems he wasn't exactly assiduous in his parliamentary duties. More naturally a scholar than a politician, he leaves one of the world's greatest libraries as his legacy.

Gosport Ferry

On the western side of Portsmouth Harbour sits the town of Gosport, a town which was once home to a remarkable range of naval and military bases, not least the Royal Naval Hospital at Haslar. At one point, early in the seventeenth century, it was even briefly mooted that Portsmouth's naval Dockyard should be relocated to the Gosport side of the harbour.

In many ways, Gosport and Portsmouth developed in tandem, suffering similar social pressures and challenges; in more recent years, both have had to find ways to cope with the significant retraction of their military establishments.

The history of the town and the history of the city are therefore inextricably linked – which in part explains the importance of linking them physically. In the 1930s, a tunnel under the harbour was proposed between the two, though the idea didn't get very far. Today, the choice remains the same as it ever did: either you take a 12-mile drive around the northern edge of the harbour through Fareham and Portchester or you take the sea crossing known as the Gosport ferry.

It's a short journey with a colourful history. As early as 1602, the whole business was fraught with argument: who actually owned the ferry? Gosport itself or the boatmen? In response, a commission was set up to control the crossing, but the arguments continued, particularly during moments of intense naval activity when the boatmen charged huge fares for getting hurried naval officers to their ships on time, very often ferrying them in boats that were barely seaworthy.

Things were regularised with the launch of a ferry service known as the floating bridge in 1840, linking Portsea Island with mainland Gosport, replacing a service for horses and light carriages which had been inaugurated in 1834. Pulled on chains and capable of taking twenty cars at a time, the floating bridge operated between Gosport and Broad Street in Portsmouth until 1959. The current service – for foot passengers, cyclists and motorcyclists – sees two ferries criss-crossing at peak times, a lone ferry operating off-peak. Its Portsmouth terminus is a pontoon bridge next to the railway station.

The ferry, slightly surprisingly, gets a mention in David Nobbs' comic novel *The Fall and Rise of Reginald Perrin* (1975). In the book, Uncle Percy Spillinger remarks disparagingly of David Harris-Jones:

> *He's a nancy-boy. A/c–D/c. He reminds me of a purser I knew on the Portsmouth–Gosport ferry. Wore coloured pants.*

PORTSMOUTH PEOPLE

Charles Dickens –
Portsmouth's Greatest Son

A literary giant not just in Britain but around the globe, Charles Dickens (1812–1870) was born at Mile End Terrace, Landport, Portsmouth, the first house in a brand-new terrace of four – a property bought by the Portsmouth Corporation in 1903 and opened on 22 July 1904 as the Dickens Birthplace Museum. Charles was the second child and first son of John Dickens, an assistant clerk in the navy pay office. He had been stationed in Portsmouth since 1808. Charles' mother was Elizabeth, née Barrow.

The family left Mile End Terrace when Dickens was only four months old as part of a famously unsettled childhood. The young Dickens lived at fourteen different addresses in as many years. From Mile End Terrace, they moved to Hawke Street for eighteen months, and then to Wish Street, Southsea,

for a year. They then moved to London for two years before John Dickens' work took him and the rest of the family to Kent.

Charles Dickens went on to create some of the most memorable characters in fiction in a succession of novels which overflowed not just with life but also the social evils of his day. The novels stand not just on their supreme literary merit, but also as detailed portraits of a society in need of reform. Dickens depicted Victorian England at every level and enjoyed huge celebrity in his own lifetime, appealing to rich and poor alike.

Dickens first gained recognition with the serial publication of *The Pickwick Papers* (1836), and many of his subsequent novels appeared in similar fashion, cliff-hangers on which the nation waited. *Oliver Twist* (1837–1839), *David Copperfield* (1849–1850), *Bleak House* (1852–1853), *A Tale of Two Cities* (1859) and *Great Expectations* (1860–1861) are among the greatest works of Victorian fiction, but even more influential perhaps was his 1843 novella *A Christmas Carol*, a powerful and enduring tale of redemption which has inspired countless adaptations across almost all the art forms ever since.

Dickens sets several chapters of *The Life and Adventures of Nicholas Nickleby* (1838–1839) in Portsmouth, and also refers to the town in *Great Expectations*. However, one of his most vivid portraits of Portsmouth comes in an essay which carries the town's name in the first volume of *All the Year Round* in 1859. Dickens captures a flavour of Portsmouth's naval importance:

We mount a balcony standing out into the sea-breeze... and from which you can have a capital bird's-eye view... Well, there, on your

*left, is fair 'Veeta,' the Isle of Wight, green
and round, and with the white town of Ryde
glittering in the sunlight at its fringe. There
spreads the Channel squadron before you.
HMS James Watt, HMS Hero, HMS Algiers,
HMS Royal Albert (three-decker), HMS
Agamemnon, are the liners... What a brilliant
spectacle Spithead makes with all these
vessels lying there, the sunlight glittering on
their chequered sides, the wind making their
colours fly, and in and out, round and round
the floating castles, the white-canvassed
yachts, the sea-butterflies
among the sea-eagles!*

Portsmouth underlined its pride in its greatest son
with a busy programme to mark Charles Dickens'
bicentenary in 2012.

PORTSMOUTH PLACES

A Circle of Forts

The irony is that by the time they were completed, they were no longer needed, but not for this were they known as **Palmerston's Follies**. The new forts at Portsmouth attracted the nickname because they seemed, to so many people, to be the wrong way round. They had their armaments pointing inland rather than out to sea. The reason, however, was a good one – in theory at least, a theory that was fortunately never tested. Their function was to protect Portsmouth from any land-based attack which threatened to encircle it.

The Portsmouth forts were part of a vast network of new and improved fortifications guarding the British, Irish and Channel Island coastline, particularly around military bases, in a programme promoted by the Prime Minister Lord Palmerston following the 1859 Royal Commission. By the time they were finished, they were no longer required, and their guns were considered out of date.

The Portsmouth defences included a group of four forts built in the Solent to guard the eastern approach to the harbour: Spitbank Fort, St Helen's Fort, Horse Sand Fort and No Man's Land Fort. Another group of forts was built on Portsdown Hill high above Portsmouth, their main weaponry facing inland. These forts were Fort Wallington, Fort Nelson, Fort Southwick, Fort Widley, Fort Purbrook, Crookhorn Redoubt and Farlington Redoubt.

Completing the defences were two further groups of forts, those on Portsea Island itself and those in Gosport on the western side of Portsmouth Harbour. The Portsea Island forts were already there (Fort Cumberland, Eastney Batteries, Lumps Fort, Southsea Castle, Point Battery and Hilsea Lines) but were improved as part of the programme. The Gosport forts, similarly to those on Portsdown Hill, had their guns facing away from Portsmouth as a counter to possible inland attack.

Substantial structures, many of the forts, particularly those in the Solent, remain as landmarks today; points of interest to vessels passing in and out of the harbour. Fort Nelson on Portsdown Hill is home to the Royal Armouries' national collection of artillery; nearby Fort Widley is now the Fort Widley Equestrian Centre, an approved riding and training centre. However, Crookhorn Redoubt and Farlington Redoubt were demolished in the nineteenth and twentieth centuries respectively. Fort Purbrook still exists.

In Portsmouth, itself, Fort Cumberland is in the hands of English Heritage and may be visited by pre-booked guided tour only; Hilsea Lines is now a leisure area, some of the fortifications still visible; Point Battery, close to the Round Tower at the harbour entrance, still makes impressive viewing; and the remains of Eastney Fort East, part of Eastney Batteries, are to be found in the grounds of the Royal Marines Museum.

One of our Greatest Engineers

Bridges, tunnels, dockyards and steamships: **Isambard Kingdom Brunel** (1806–1859), the Victorian era's greatest engineer and one of Portsmouth's most famous sons, built them all. Brunel was born in Portsmouth on 9 April 1806, the third child and first son of Sir Marc Isambard Brunel (1769–1849), a distinguished civil engineer whose tunnel under the River Thames between Rotherhithe and Wapping won him a knighthood.

The young Isambard was educated in Chelsea, Hove and France. Among his many achievements, Brunel designed the *Great Western*, which narrowly missed out on becoming the first ship to cross the Atlantic under steam power alone. His *Great Britain*, launched 1843, is considered by many the first modern ship, metal rather than wood, and driven by an engine rather than by wind. Brunel was also responsible for the redesign and construction of many of Britain's major docks, including Bristol, Cardiff and Milford Haven.

Placed second in 2002 in a BBC public poll to determine the 100 Greatest Britons, Brunel was also the man who created the Clifton Suspension Bridge, a symbol of Bristol still crossed by millions of vehicles a year. Brunel was project engineer but the initiative was fraught with problems, controversies and delays. He did not live to see it finished, and it was completed as his memorial.

Portsmouth's Victorian Writers

Celia Levetus née Moss (*c.*1819–1873) was born in Portsmouth, where she wrote initially with her younger sister. Their first book of poems, *Early Efforts*, was published in 1839. The volume was dedicated to Sir George Staunton MP and was subscribed to by Lord Palmerston, as well as by most of the prominent Jewish families in London. The sisters followed it with a collection of historical romances entitled *The Romance of Jewish History* (1840) and its sequel, *Tales of Jewish History* (1843). Celia later collected her own stories in *The King's Physician and other Tales* (1865).

Regarded by some as the last of the great Victorian writers, novelist and poet **George Meredith** (1828–1909) was born at 73 High Street, Portsmouth, where he had an impoverished upbringing and intermittent education in Portsmouth and Southsea, followed by boarding school in Suffolk. Meredith soon made his way into literary circles, publishing *Poems* in 1851. His first volume of fiction was *The Shaving of Shagpat: an Arabian Entertainment* (1856), and his first full-length novel was *The Ordeal of Richard Feverel: a History of Father and Son* (1859), a work typical of his tendency to work through personal trauma in his writing. The novel for which he is chiefly remembered, *The Egoist*, was published in 1879. Trying to make ends meet, he became a publisher's reader for Chapman and Hall where one of the younger writers he encouraged was Thomas Hardy. In his obituary *The Times* commented that 'in the end he achieved the position of the greatest man of letters of his age', an estimation which looks misplaced a century after his death.

Children's author and hymn writer **Sarah Doudney** (1841–1926) was born at Portsea, educated at

Madame Dowell's College in Southsea and lived for many years in Lovedean, near Catherington, about 10 miles north of Portsmouth. She started writing poetry and prose as a child, published variously in *The Churchman's Family Magazine* and in Charles Dickens' literary periodical *All the Year Round*. She developed into a prolific novelist, and is most remembered for her fiction for girls, though some of her hymns including *Saviour, now the Day is ending* are still occasionally sung. Her huge outpouring includes *Stories of Girlhood, or the Brook and the River* (1877), *Monksbury College: A Tale of Schoolgirl Life* (1878), *Faith's Revenge* (1879) and *The Scarlet Satin Petticoat* (1879). She died in Oxford.

Irish writer **John Boyle O'Reilly** (1844–1890) didn't enjoy the happiest of stays in Portsmouth. A Fenian supporting an independent Irish republic, he joined the British army in the hope of converting his fellow soldiers to the cause – and was rewarded with stints in prison in Millbank, Portsmouth and Dartmoor. He was transported to Australia in 1868, but escaped to America where he became a prominent lecturer in Irish affairs. His collections of poems include

Songs from the Southern Seas (1873) and *Songs, Legends and Ballads* (1878). His novel *Moondyne* (1879) was based on his experiences as a convict in Western Australia where it is considered a significant contribution to convict literature. He died suddenly following an overdose of his wife's sleeping medicine. It is not known whether he intended his own death or simply miscalculated.

Lady Katie Magnus née Emanuel (1844–1924) was born at 101 High Street, Portsmouth, the daughter of the first Jewish mayor of Portsmouth. She married Sir Philip Magnus in the garden of her parents' home, Grove House, Southsea. Sir Philip was minister of the West London Synagogue and MP for London University, but Katie Magnus made her own career, firstly as a teacher at the Portsmouth Sabbath school and synagogue – the trigger for a literary output which was mostly educational in intent. *About the Jews in Bible Times* was published in 1881; *Outlines of Jewish History* appeared in 1886. She worked tirelessly to increase the educational opportunities for girls from poor Jewish families in London.

Rudyard Kipling (1865–1936), author of works including *The Jungle Book* (1894), *Kim* (1901) and *Just So Stories* (1902), was born in Bombay. His first taste of England was in Southsea where he endured the childhood unhappiness which was to act as a spur to his writing. Kipling and his sister were sent to live with Captain Pryse Agar Holloway and his wife Sarah at Lorne Lodge at 4 Campbell Road, Southsea (marked today with a blue plaque). The couple boarded the children of British nationals serving in India, but for the young Rudyard it proved a miserable experience – a time of neglect and unhappiness. In *Something of Myself* (1937) he wrote:

It was an establishment run with the full vigour of the Evangelical as revealed to the Woman. I had never heard of Hell, so I was introduced to it in all its terrors – I and whatever luckless little slavey might be in the house, whom severe rationing had led to steal food. [...] If you cross-examine a child of seven or eight on his day's doings (specially when he wants to go to sleep) he will contradict himself very satisfactorily. If each contradiction be set

*down as a lie and retailed at breakfast, life
is not easy. I have known a certain amount
of bullying, but this was calculated torture
– religious as well as scientific. Yet it made
me give attention to the lies I soon found it
necessary to tell: and this, I presume, is the
foundation of literary effort.*

SOMETHING OF MYSELF (MACMILLAN, 1937)
CHAPTER I: A VERY YOUNG PERSON 1865–1878

Herbert George Wells (1866–1946) won legions of
fans for his science-fiction writing, including *The
Time Machine* (1895), *The Island of Doctor Moreau*
(1896), *The Invisible Man* (1897) and, perhaps most
notably, *The War of the Worlds* (1898). Book One was
entitled *The Coming of the Martians*; Book Two, *The
Earth under the Martians*. Put them together, and
the work, one of the first to pit man against extra-
terrestrial forces, set the standard for subsequent sci-
fi invasion literature, spawning a string of imitations
and adaptations.

In more realistic mode, Wells was also the author
of *Kipps* (1905) – a novel directly born of his
unhappy time in Southsea where he worked from

1881 to 1883 as a draper's apprentice at Hyde's,
^the Southsea Drapery Emporium. Long hours and
^dormitory accommodation helped convince him of
the inequalities of wealth distribution in Victorian
England – something which led him to stand as the
Labour Party candidate for London University in the
1922 and 1923 general elections.

Portsmouth Dockyard in the Twentieth Century

In 1900 Portsmouth Dockyard employed around 8,000 men, a figure which doubled in the 14 years which took Britain to the brink of the First World War. As European conflict loomed, Portsmouth stood certain of its global significance:

> *The visits of foreign fleets and squadrons make Portsmouth a dispenser of national hospitality, and the grand naval displays of the Jubilee and the Coronation are the climax and the complement of the national pageants which we share with London alone.*
>
> Charpentier's Guide to Portsmouth and Southsea (1913)

Around 1,200 ships were refitted in Portsmouth during the 1914–1918 war, but inevitably with peace the numbers of men employed in the Dockyard began to fall, slipping back to around 12,000 in the 1920s before rising again in the 1930s against a background of yet more European uncertainty. The Second World War closed with Dockyard employment at an all-time high, around the 25,000 mark.

Once again, peace saw the numbers fall away rapidly, particularly during the 1960s, and then came a hammer blow. In the early 1980s a defence review under the then Conservative Secretary of State for Defence, John Nott, concluded that of the four home dockyards, the country could afford to close both Chatham and Portsmouth. In the end, Portsmouth won a concession. Rather than closure, it was reconstituted (and downgraded) as a naval base.

The timing could not have been worse. Portsmouth soon found itself once again at the centre of world events when Argentine forces invaded and occupied the Falkland Islands and South Georgia on 2 April 1982. The British government's response was to dispatch a naval task force from Portsmouth, ironically at a time when the process of downgrading Portsmouth Dockyard had already begun. Ships from Portsmouth had been an important part of the fleet that drove off the Spanish Armada in 1588; four centuries later, there were emotional scenes as ships sailed from Portsmouth to the Falklands, some never to return.

The conflict lasted 74 days at a cost of 255 British military dead and 649 Argentinian. Portsmouth had yet again responded in the country's hour of need.

The Battle of Trafalgar is the sea battle most readily connected with Portsmouth, but the Battle of Jutland in the First World War had the greater impact on the city. Historians will tell you that relatively few of the men who fought or died at Trafalgar had strong links with Portsmouth. However, the battle fought on 31 May and 1 June 1916 in the North Sea off the coast of Denmark exacted a heavy toll on the city.

W. G. Gates, editor of the city's *Evening News*, said: 'Sorrow hung like a pall over the city for weeks.' The Battle of Jutland was the largest naval battle in the First World War; its outcome meant that it was also the last. Total killed and wounded were just under 10,000; just over 3,000 were German, but nearly 7,000 were British and of those the majority were in some way connected to Portsmouth.

The World's Greatest Detective

From the mind of a struggling young Southsea doctor came the greatest detective the world has ever known; the legendary Sherlock Holmes, a mighty figure who still captures the imagination and inspires film and television adaptations more than a century later.

Sir Arthur Conan Doyle (1859–1930) first set up in practice as a doctor at 1 Bush Villas, Elm Grove, Southsea in 1882, and at first, patients were few and far between – though he forced himself to remain cheerful.

> *No patients yet but the number of people who stop and read my plate is enormous. On Wednesday evening in 25 minutes 28 people stopped in front of it, and yesterday I counted 24 in 15 minutes, which was better still. On the average of one a minute of working hours 2,880 people have read it during the week.*

LETTER TO MOTHER, QUOTED IN *ARTHUR CONAN DOYLE: A LIFE IN LETTERS*, EDITED BY JON LELLENBERG, DANIEL STASHOWER, CHARLES FOLEY (HARPER, 2007)

Conan Doyle sought to save face:

> *I have to sit up nearly to midnight every night in order to polish my two door-plates without being seen. Have no gas yet.*

IBID.

More importantly, he used his time well. As he waited, so often in vain, so he would write. My proud boast is that my great-grandmother, whom I never met, claimed she saw him scribbling away in his empty consulting room. And so the character of Sherlock Holmes started to emerge, modelled in part on Dr Joseph Bell, under whom Conan Doyle had studied medicine at Edinburgh University.

1 Bush Villas, Elm Grove, Southsea was destroyed by German bombing during World War Two. A blue plaque, attached to a block of flats, now marks the site and claims both Conan Doyle and Holmes as Portsmouth's own. The inscription notes:

While he lived in Portsmouth, Conan Doyle threw himself into the life of the City. He joined the local Portsmouth Literary and Scientific Society, gave numerous speeches on topics of the day, and played for the local cricket and bowls teams, as well as being the first goalkeeper for what is now Portsmouth Football Club.

While in Southsea, Conan Doyle wrote the first two Sherlock Holmes novels, *A Study in Scarlet* (1887) and *The Sign of Four* (1890). Portsmouth was, in this sense, the birthplace of the world's greatest fictional detective. Conan Doyle left Southsea in December 1890. Holmes features in two further novels, *The Hound of the Baskervilles* and *The Valley of Fear*, serialised in *The Strand Magazine* in 1901–1902 and 1914–1915 respectively. There are also five collections of short stories: *The Adventures of Sherlock Holmes* (1891–1892), *The Memoirs of Sherlock Holmes* (1892–1893), *The Return of Sherlock Holmes* (1903–1904), *The Reminiscences of Sherlock Holmes* (1908–1913 and 1917) and *The Case-Book of Sherlock Holmes* (1921–1927).

How did Portsmouth Become Pompey?

Pompey: A nickname for the town and dockyards at Portsmouth, and specifically for Portsmouth Football Club.

OXFORD DICTIONARY OF MODERN SLANG
(OXFORD UNIVERSITY PRESS, 2010)

How Portsmouth – and indeed Portsmouth FC – became Pompey is a question which will never satisfactorily be resolved. Far more enjoyable is simply to enjoy the various, often fanciful attempts at explaining it.

The Oxford Companion to Ships and the Sea (2006) records Pompey as British sailors' slang for the city:

It is not known how or when the name came into being, though one theory is that it owes

*its origin to the fact that the local fire brigade,
known by their French name pompiers, used
to exercise on Southsea Common,
adjacent to Portsmouth.*

But there are plenty of other possibilities to savour, some of them linked to the alcohol which generally flowed fairly freely through the city. Try to say Portsmouth Point when you are 'four sheets to the wind', as a sailor might say, and it might just come out as Pompey.

Another, more sober, possible derivation is the fact that navigational charts used to record Portsmouth Point as Pom. P. Hence Pompey. Unless, of course, the word Pompey derives from the pomp of this grand naval city, a city which is therefore pomp-y. Equally, Pompey could be a corruption of the word Bombay: a bizarre theory suggests that Portuguese sailors saw a resemblance between Portsmouth and the Indian city.

Or perhaps the nickname Pompey was brought back by the group of Portsmouth-based sailors who climbed Pompey's Pillar near Alexandria in Egypt in around 1781 and won the name for themselves, the 'Pompey Boys'. Maybe the word Pompey has something to do with Pompeii – a possibility put forward by those who note the Roman origins of

Portchester. Maybe more likely is that Pompey comes from *La Pompée*, a captured French ship which was moored in the harbour as a floating prison around the turn of the eighteenth century.

Implausible as it is, however, there is something irresistible about the tale which tells of a drunken sailor who fell asleep during a lecture on the Roman Empire given by Dame Agnes Weston, founder of the Royal Sailors' Rests. When the good Dame said that the Emperor Pompey had died, the slumbering sailor roused himself to a minimum level of consciousness, just sufficient to voice the commiseration: 'Poor old Pompey!' Quite how Pompey then became a nickname for Portsmouth isn't recorded. Maybe it's best simply to enjoy the story.

Portsmouth's Men and Women of Science

Portsmouth's literary importance has long been acknowledged. So too should its contribution to science and learning.

As titles go, it hardly trips off the tongue, but the research it contained was certainly important in its time. Mathematician **Thomas Haselden** was a naval schoolmaster, serving as headmaster of the Royal Academy at Portsmouth. In 1722 he published his *Description and use of... that most excellent invention commonly call'd Mercator's chart, to which is added the description of a new scale whereby distances may*

be measured at one extent of a pair of compasses. He died in Portsmouth in May 1740.

Did he really look up to the stars and see the French Revolution looming? It seems that he genuinely did – not that it did his own cause much good. The astrologer, physician and writer on the occult **Ebenezer Sibly** (1751–*c.*1799) was destined to die in obscurity where he has remained ever since.

Sibly was born in Bristol, but it was in Portsmouth that he made his mark. He was initiated into freemasonry in the city and completed his first book, *A New and Complete Illustration of the Celestial Science of Astrology.* Published in four parts (1784–1788), it was a massive compendium of astrology, occult philosophy and magic. Fascinated by mesmerism and by the links he saw between ancient magic and modern science, Sibly was also the author of *A Key to Physic and the Occult Sciences* (1794). One of his stranger achievements came in 1787 when he studied the movement of the sun to predict the French Revolution:

Here is every prospect... that some very important event will happen in the politics of France, such as may dethrone, or very nearly touch the life of, the king, and make victims of many great and illustrious men in church and state, preparatory to a revolution... which will at once astonish and surprise the surrounding nations.

On 4 October 1784 balloonist and chemist **James Sadler** (*c.*1753–1828) made the first ascent by any English aeronaut, with a 170-foot hot-air balloon he had built himself, rising from Oxford to a height of 3,600 feet and landing six miles away, half an hour later. Sadler's technical skills were briefly put to use as barracks master at Portsmouth in 1795.

One of the founding fathers of modern British ophthalmology, the surgeon and oculist **James Ware**

(1756–1815) was born in Portsmouth, attended Portsmouth Grammar School and was apprenticed to the surgeon of the King's Yard in Portsmouth, continuing his studies at St Thomas's Hospital, London. A noted humanitarian, he was one of the founders of the Society for the Relief of the Widows and Orphans of Medical Men in London and also founded a school for the indigent blind. More importantly, he spread awareness of the importance of ophthalmic surgery, which had yet to establish itself as a respectable branch of medicine. His publications included *Remarks on the Ophthalmy, Psorophthalmy and Purulent Eye* (1780) and his two-volume *Chirurgical Observations Relative to the Eye* (1805).

Irish-born physician and surgeon **James Johnson** (1777–1845) became a surgeon's mate in the navy and later full surgeon on a number of voyages, most notably to the Far East. Johnson published an account of the expedition as *The Oriental Voyager, or, Descriptive sketches and cursory remarks on a voyage to India and China in His Majesty's ship Caroline, performed in the years 1803-4-5-6* (1807).

Alert to the effects on both himself and his fellow servicemen, he published *The Influence of Tropical Climates on European Constitutions* in 1812. After the end of the French wars in 1814, Johnson worked as a general practitioner in Portsmouth, launching his *Medico-Chirurgical Review*. He moved to London in 1818. Other works included *Economy of Health, or, The stream of human life with reflections on the septennial phases of human existence* (1836).

Army officer and military surgeon **John Hennen** (1779–1828) studied medicine in Edinburgh, joined the Shropshire militia as assistant surgeon and served throughout the Peninsular War in various regiments. For his work after Waterloo, he was appointed deputy inspector of hospitals and placed on the home staff at Portsmouth. Hennen distilled his thoughts and the fruits of his years of service into his *Observations on some important points in the practice of military surgery, and in the arrangement and police of hospitals* (1818). In 1826 he became principal medical officer at Gibraltar where he died of fever.

Astronomer **William Bayly**, who had become assistant in 1766 to the astronomer royal Nevil Maskelyne at the Royal Observatory, Greenwich, was appointed headmaster of the Royal Naval Academy in Portsmouth Dockyard in 1785 where he remained until 1807. However, his final years in Portsmouth were desperately sad. He lost his wife and seven children to consumption and a midshipman son to naval action before his own death in Portsmouth on 21 December 1810.

The pioneering Plymouth-born nurse **Martha Jane Loane** (1852–1933) did much to raise awareness of public health issues – while practising a little literary deception on the side. Young Martha spent part of her childhood in Portsmouth before boarding at the Royal Naval School for Females in Middlesex. After hospital nursing, she moved into district nursing, a new branch of nursing focusing on treating patients in their own homes. In 1897 Martha became the superintendent of Queen's Nurses for the Borough of Portsmouth Association for Nursing the Sick Poor. In retirement a string of nursing handbooks were published in her name, including *The District Nurse as Health Missioner*, *The Duties of a Superintendent in a Small Home for District Nurses* and *The Incidental Opportunities of District Nursing*, all in 1904. However, in fact it was Martha's younger half-sister **Alice Eliza Loane** (1863–1922) who compiled and wrote the works, gaining recognition only posthumously. Alice was born at 2 Exbury Place, Green Road, Southsea, and published much of her writing under the name M. Loane.

She helped nurse Mrs Pankhurst and other hunger-striking suffragettes; she also created a fan to dispel poison gas in the trenches of the First World War. **Hertha Ayrton** (1854–1923), women's campaigner, inventor and electrical engineer, was truly a remarkable woman.

She was born Phoebe Sarah Marks, the daughter of a watchmaker, at 6 Queen Street, Portsea, on 28 April 1854, and remained in the city until the age of nine when she attended her aunts' school in north-west

London. From 1877 to 1881, Hertha – a nickname she adopted after the heroine of an Algernon Charles Swinburne poem that criticised organised religion – read mathematics at Girton College, Cambridge, where she also found time to set up a fire brigade, lead the choral society and construct a pulse recorder. She married the electrical engineer William Edward Ayrton and in London lectured to women on electricity and its domestic possibilities. A friend of Marie Curie, she published her research in twelve papers in *The Electrician* (1895–1896). Her book *The Electric Arc* (1902) became the standard work on the subject. She later patented anti-aircraft searchlights, developed for the Admiralty.

Ayrton was also a passionate member of the women's movement, supporting the militant suffragettes. Among numerous other achievements, she helped set up the International Federation of University Women in 1919 and the National Union of Scientific Workers in 1920.

The successful flight of the Wright brothers in December 1903 was all the inspiration **Sir Edwin Alliott Verdon Roe** (1877–1958) needed to devote himself to powered flight. A pioneer English pilot and aircraft manufacturer, he contributed an article to the engineering supplement of *The Times* (24 January 1906), to which the editor felt obliged to add: 'All attempts at artificial aviation on the basis he describes are not only dangerous to life, but foredoomed to failure from an engineering standpoint.' Five years later Roe had founded the Avro company (A. V. Roe & Co.) and – the perfect riposte to the disbelief he had met with earlier – designed the first enclosed-cabin aeroplane. In October 1912, the plane established a British flying record of seven and a half hours. Roe made his home at Long Meadow in Rowlands Castle and died at St Mary's Hospital, Portsmouth, on 4 January 1958.

Aerodynamicist **Arthur Fage** (1890–1977) was born in Portsmouth, the younger son of a dockyard coppersmith. Fage became an apprentice shipwright at Portsmouth Dockyard before winning a royal exhibition to the Royal College of Science, South Kensington, where he specialised in mechanics. He joined the National Physical Laboratory, Teddington, where he pursued his interest in aeronautics. His popular success was the book *The Aeroplane* (1915) which he followed with the more technical *Airscrews in Theory and Experiment* (1920). He carried out important work in the field of turbulence and also high-speed aerodynamics.

The first and so far only female Lord Mayor of London (1983–1984), **Mary Donaldson, Baroness Donaldson of Lymington** (1921–2003) was born at The Square, Wickham, just north of Portsmouth and educated at Portsmouth High School, before training as a nurse. Donaldson was closely involved with cancer charities, serving as chairman of the Women's National Cancer Control Campaign from 1967 to 1969 and vice-president of the British Cancer Council in 1970. She also served as chairman of the voluntary (later interim) licensing authority for human in vitro fertilisation and embryology, set up by the Medical Research Council and the Royal College of Obstetricians and Gynaecologists.

The Internet can be traced back directly to the work of computer scientist **Donald Watts Davies** (1924–2000), one of the inventors of packet-switched computer networking. Davies was born in Glamorgan, but when his father died, his mother brought her young family back to her home city of Portsmouth. Donald attended Portsmouth's Southern Secondary School for Boys before going on to study physics at London's Imperial College, later becoming involved with the early development of computers. He joined the National Physical Laboratory and worked briefly with Alan Turing. His greatest achievement came in the mid-1960s with his work on a fast message-switching service to achieve efficient communication between computers – a project which laid the groundwork for what became the Internet.

Portsmouth's Historic Theatres

Portsmouth is home to two theatres, both now at differing stages in their bids to return to past glories. Both were the product of the business sense of John Waters Boughton and – to differing degrees – the architectural vision of Frank Matcham, one of Britain's greatest theatre designers.

The Theatre Royal opened in 1954 – thirty years prior to the opening of the nearby Guildhall – but Boughton had bigger plans for it. Working with C. J. Phipps, he undertook a major rebuild of the venue, re-opening it as the **New Theatre Royal** in

1884 before remodelling it again in 1900, this time working with Matcham.

It enjoyed a degree of success in those early days, but sadly much of the venue's history has been somewhat chequered. From 1932 to 1948 it served as a cinema, before becoming a variety theatre and then closing altogether in 1955. The 1960s saw it used for bingo, wrestling and squatting – with the threat of demolition hanging over it.

Things looked up in 1970 when the Theatre Royal Society was formed, and in 1971 Ken Russell filmed *The Boy Friend* there, starring Twiggy. But in 1972, a disastrous fire destroyed the stage, the fly tower and the technical block. A temporary thrust stage was installed in the 1980s, and in 2004 the venue, with much reduced capacity, was reopened after extensive refurbishment.

It slowly rebuilt its reputation and will be redeveloped in a multi-million pound scheme in collaboration with the University of Portsmouth. The hope is to return the theatre to past glories and add the Anthony Minghella Creative Learning Space, offering a nineteenth-century heritage auditorium with a twenty-first-century stage house.

Meanwhile, after years of uncertainty, the **Kings** is reclaiming its crown on the back of refurbishment and strong audiences. If nothing particularly magical is happening on stage, just look up and around you. Southsea's Kings Theatre is one of the best examples of an elegant Edwardian playhouse to be found in Britain, with a wealth of original features.

After Matcham's remodelling of the New Theatre Royal in 1900, he and Boughton began to hatch plans for a new Drama and Opera House in Southsea. From these plans emerged the Kings, opening on 30 September 1907.

The venue in Albert Road played an important morale-boosting role in the city during the Second World War with a busy programme of concerts; and the venue always attracted the biggest names in the acting world including Sarah Bernhardt, Rex Harrison, Noël Coward, Ivor Novello and Sybil Thorndike.

However, the later years of the twentieth century were a difficult time for the theatre – years which saw a valiant campaign to keep the venue open. In 2001, the Kings was bought by Portsmouth City Council and leased to the Kings Theatre Trust Ltd which today holds responsibility both for the upkeep of the building and the shows it puts on. The Trust has overseen the running of the theatre since 2003. Actresses Kate O'Mara, Dillie Keane and Lisa Riley are the theatre's patrons.

Alongside Portsmouth Guildhall, Portsmouth's major music venues are the Pyramids Centre and the Wedgewood Rooms. Together, the venues cater for all tastes, bringing a wide range of music to the city.

Other Portsmouths

Not surprisingly, given both Portsmouth's importance and also the obvious derivation of its name, Portsmouth, Hampshire isn't the only Portsmouth in the world. The United States of America boast no fewer than four.

Portsmouth, New Hampshire, is the state's only seaport and oldest settlement. Originally it was named Piscataqua after the Piscataqua River on which it was established in 1623, but the name was soon changed to Strawbery Banke – which didn't last long as a designation either. The community settled on the name Portsmouth in 1653. Like the

UK original, it is a port at a river mouth. The town served as the seat of New Hampshire's provincial government until the American Revolution. For most of the twentieth century it was a centre for the building and repair of submarines. It is now predominantly an agricultural and resort region with light manufacturing industries. The population in 2010 was 20,779.

Founded in 1638 by William Coddington, John Clarke, Anne Hutchinson, and associates from the Massachusetts Bay colony, **Portsmouth, Rhode Island** began life as Pocasset, an Algonquian name referring to the width of the Sakonnet River along which it lies. It became a town in 1640 and its name was changed to Portsmouth. It is now an outlying suburb of Newport city. Industry includes the manufacture of electronic equipment and boatbuilding. Tourism is also important. The population in 2010 was 17,389.

The city and port of **Portsmouth, Virginia**, lies on the south shore of the Elizabeth River, opposite the city of Norfolk. It was founded in 1752 and named after the English city port. During the American Revolution, the town was occupied alternately by British and American troops. Today, Portsmouth forms part of the important US military complex at Hampton Roads. The main economic activities are shipbuilding and repair in the port's navy yard, officially called the Norfolk Naval Shipyard. The population in 2010 was 95,535.

Portsmouth, Ohio was founded in 1803 and named by land speculator Major Henry Massie after Portsmouth, Virginia, hometown of his friend Josiah Shackford. Portsmouth, Ohio, lies along the Ohio River at the mouth of the Scioto River. Early prosperity was encouraged by the opening of the Ohio and Erie Canal in 1832, a development which made Portsmouth a point of transfer from canal barges to river packets. With the decline of steamboats, the city emerged as an important railway centre. It is now protected by a 23-metre floodwall following disastrous river floods in 1937. The population in 2010 was 20,226.

Portsmouth's Painters

Portsmouth's coastal location and its naval importance have long encouraged the artistic temperament.

A painter of miniatures and a publisher, **Robert Bowyer** (1758–1834) was born in Portsmouth. At first he worked as a clerk to a merchant in Portsmouth and then later in London where painting became his calling. After professional training, he exhibited first at the Free Society of Artists in 1782 and then at the Royal Academy in 1783. His success as a miniaturist grew strongly, with patrons including the Duke of Rutland and Lord Nelson.

The son of a purser in the navy, Portsmouth-born painter and illustrator **Henry Thomson** (1773–1843) was encouraged from an early age by his father who took him to Paris in 1787 and then later on an extended tour of the continent. Thomson began to exhibit at the Royal Academy. Portraits and mythological and domestic subjects were his strengths; important works include *The Infancy of Jupiter* (1812) and *Eurydice* (1814). Thomson was appointed Keeper of the Royal Academy in 1825.

Edinburgh-born marine painter **John Christian Schetky** (1778–1874) became professor of drawing at the Royal Naval Academy in Portsmouth in 1811. He stayed there until the college closed as a young officer training establishment in 1836, and was then appointed to a similar post in Addiscombe, Kent, from which he retired in 1855. His career was distinguished by royal commissions from George IV, William IV and Queen Victoria. He also commemorated a number of historic sea battles and events including the Battle of Trafalgar in 1805 and the sinking of the *Royal George* at Spithead in 1782. Attention to detail and close observation are seen as his hallmarks.

He wasn't in Portsmouth by choice, but it was his stay in Portsmouth that set **Ambroise-Louis Garneray** (1783–1857) on his path to becoming an artist. It was during the Napoleonic War, while he was held captive in a prison hulk in Portsmouth Harbour, that Garneray began to paint. When he finally returned to France, he studied art under his father who was a professional painter. In 1817 he was appointed marine painter to the Duc d'Angoulême, Admiral of France.

Joseph Francis Gilbert (1792–1855) exhibited landscape and figures at the Royal Academy while living at 137 High Street, Portsmouth. He moved to Chichester where he remained for many years, drawing his artistic inspiration from the Sussex landscape. He died in London.

Marine painter and naval officer **Richard Brydges Beechey** (1808–1895) entered the Royal Naval College at Portsmouth in 1821, going on to serve as midshipman on HMS *Blossom*, a ship commanded by his brother, Captain Frederick William Beechey. Frederick chronicled their journey to the South Seas and north to the Bering Strait; Richard provided the illustrations. Richard was promoted captain in 1857 and retired in 1864 to concentrate on an artistic career which was now flourishing. Between 1832 and 1877 he exhibited seascapes nearly every year at key London venues including the Royal Academy and the British Institution. Regarded by some as the best painter the navy ever produced, Beechey died at his home, 9 Portland Terrace, Southsea, on 8 March 1895.

George Cole (1810–1883) was a landscape and animal artist who began his professional life with no formal education as a ship's painter at Portsmouth. Marriage to Eliza Vicat, daughter of George and Catherine Vicat of Cosham, may have been the turning point, as from then his star rose. The 1840s saw him exhibiting in London, a decade which also saw him develop his skills as an animal painter in the manner of Edwin Landseer and Thomas Sidney Cooper. He later focused on landscape, working alongside his son George Vicat Cole in the early 1850s. After a brief argument, however, they never worked together again.

The engraver **John Richardson Jackson** (1819–1877) was born in Portsmouth. He came to prominence in 1847 with his engraving *The Otter and Salmon*; regular work followed, predominantly as an engraver of portraits with occasional landscapes. He exhibited regularly over a number of years at the Royal Academy where his portraits included Queen Victoria and the Princess Royal and her sisters. Jackson died at Southsea on 10 May 1877.

Hampshire, Surrey, Yorkshire, Wales and Ireland were among the inspirations for watercolour painter **George Shalders** (*c.*1825–1873), who was born in Portsmouth. Shalders exhibited in London at the Royal Academy and at the Society of British Artists, becoming an associate of the New Society of Painters in Water Colours. Overwork is said to have contributed to his early death.

Landscape painter **George Vicat Cole** (1833–1893) was the eldest of five children born to noted Portsmouth artist George Cole. Born in Portsmouth, he adopted his mother's French Huguenot maiden name to distinguish him from his father. Later, he dropped the George altogether and used Vicat as his first name. At the age of 20, he had two works accepted by the Royal Academy. In the 1860s he was heavily influenced by the Pre-Raphaelites; his focus was increasingly on the Surrey landscape and later also on Sussex. Subsequent works included a series of paintings of the Thames. Like his father, he was buried in Kensal Green cemetery, London.

London-born artist and writer **William Lionel Wyllie** (1851–1931) showed early talent, first exhibiting at the Royal Academy in 1868. It was his love of the sea that defined his work. Wyllie became a member of the Royal Academy in 1907, the year in which he moved to a house overlooking the entrance to Portsmouth Harbour. British naval history attracted him increasingly, and as a founder member of the Society for Nautical Research he was instrumental in the campaign to have HMS *Victory* restored to her former glory. His panorama of the Battle of Trafalgar was unveiled by George V in Portsmouth Dockyard in 1930. He was buried in the churchyard within Portchester Castle.

Few people have done more to promote photography as an art form than photographer, writer, and editor **Francis James Mortimer** (1874–1944), who was born at 9 Ordnance Row, Portsea. A pupil at Portsmouth Grammar School, Mortimer at first seemed destined for a career in law, but when the law firm which employed him went bust, he opted instead for journalism, design and photography. In the closing years of the nineteenth century, his cartoons featured in a variety of publications. More perilously, trying to photograph the sea off the Scilly Islands, he would tie a lifeline around himself and frequently lose his camera as the waves crashed around him. In 1902 Mortimer moved to London where he pursued his journalistic and photographic interests, generally combining the two. In 1908 he became editor of the merged *Amateur Photographer and Photographic News*, and in his remaining years edited a wide variety of books on the subject of photography and exhibited frequently.

As the *Oxford Dictionary of National Biography* notes: 'Mortimer worked tirelessly as an editor, writer, photographer, exhibitor, and judge, establishing photography's credentials not only in Britain but also around the world.'

Welsh-born painter and illustrator **Nina Hamnett** (1890–1956) took classes at the Portsmouth School of Art in 1903, after which her family settled in London where she continued her studies at the London School of Art. Flamboyant and at times outrageous, she became known as the Queen of Bohemia, once dancing nude on a Montparnasse cafe table just for 'the hell of it'. Revelling in the avant-garde in both London and Paris, she honed her own individual style and made an important contribution to the Modern Movement. She declared: 'My ambition is to paint psychological portraits that shall represent accurately the spirit of the age'. Her death was tragically grim. She fell out of the window of her flat at 164 Westbourne Terrace, Paddington, and was impaled on the railings below. Whether it was suicide or simply drunkenness was never resolved.

Sculptor **Frank Graeme Martin** (1914–2004) was born in Portsmouth and attended Portsmouth Art School before studying in London. He served with distinction during the Second World War, twice being mentioned in dispatches for bravery during the Anzio landings. After the war Martin lived for many years at Hayling Island, where he returned to sculpture, creating works including a number of life-sized standing figures in terracotta. Martin was appointed head of sculpture at St Martin's School of Art in London in 1952 and remained there until 1979.

The British painter, sculptor, designer and pop artist **Derek Boshier** was born in Portsmouth in 1937. He attended the Royal College of Art in London from 1959 to 1962 where his contemporaries included David Hockney and R. B. Kitaj. Many of his works of the early 1960s were concerned with the manipulative power of advertising, treating human figures as if they were mass-produced goods; others looked at the space race and Britain's relationship with the USA. Time in India saw him introduce Hindu symbolism into his work; later he moved towards hard-edged geometrical abstracts. In 1979 he took up painting again and taught painting throughout the 1980s at the University of Texas. Boshier now lives in Los Angeles.

British potter **Grayson Perry** made his mark when he won the Turner Prize in 2003. Controversy, as so often with the Turner Prize, wasn't far behind – and not because he was the first potter to win it. Dressing openly as a transvestite, Perry often inscribes his work with images and messages reflecting dark themes including domestic violence and child abuse – an approach which he describes as a 'guerrilla tactic'. Born in 1960 in Chelmsford, Essex, he studied at Portsmouth Polytechnic.

PORTSMOUTH PLACES

'A seaside resort
blessed by Nature'

*Southsea – a seaside resort blessed by Nature
with thousands of advantages and joys. There
is advantage in being sheltered at all on this
southern coast to which spring comes first and
on which summer sunshine lingers longest.*

The Official Guide to Southsea, published
by Portsmouth Corporation (1928)

Southsea is Portsmouth's pride, its very own resort.
Of course, you would expect the city to blow its
own trumpet, but the *Southsea and Portsmouth
Official Guide* of 1919 certainly makes for colourful
reading. Labelling Southsea as nothing less than 'the
Gateway to the Empire', it promises: 'No one who
visits or resides in Southsea need spend a single dull
moment'. The city's commemorative guide marking

the Coronation of George V in 1911 waxes positively lyrical about 'Sunny Southsea: The Gem of Seaside Resorts', hailing it not simply 'The Brightest Spot on the South Coast' but also 'The Centre of Health and Sunshine!' 'The Premier Watering Place of England', it is 'uniquely situated facing the Silvery Solent, sheltered on the North by a Range of Hills.'

Southsea is essentially a place for those who prefer their seaside stay to be spent amid surroundings that are peaceful, quiet and refined without being dull; for children whose helplessness and venturesomeness demand absolute safety, as far as natural conditions go; and for all anxious to recruit the fagged body and mind; and above all for the lovers of the glorious sea and its never-ending charms, and those who like to lounge on the beautiful greensward adjoining Southsea Castle.

SOUTHSEA AND PORTSMOUTH CORONATION SOUVENIR GUIDE, ISSUED FREE BY THE SOUTHSEA AND PORTSMOUTH ENTERTAINMENT COMMITTEE (JUNE 1911)

Southsea has long been proud of its health-giving qualities:

Portsmouth appeals to the million – the mirthful crowds of busy workers from the great centres of industry as well as the numerous classes who desire restfulness with adequate diversion. It is a blithe and heartsome place to the workworn on whom it seems to exercise a potent spell, almost magical in its effects. The depressed in spirit breathes its wonderful air tonic, and the cloud of ill-health or worry is dispelled like an early morning mist, the dyspeptic suddenly regains the forgotten joys of eating, and the morose becomes infected with the gaiety and vivacity of a well-ordered, fascinating and salubrious resort.

IBID.

The 1919 guide specifies – albeit in passing – a significant advantage Southsea possessed over Portsmouth itself:

Unlike its neighbour Portsmouth, Southsea is of comparatively modern origin, which fact confers the advantage that the houses are

built on concrete in beds in which the drains
are laid. It is thus comparatively secure from
epidemics of enteric fever.
SOUTHSEA AND PORTSMOUTH OFFICIAL GUIDE
(1919)

The great Sir Arthur Conan Doyle, so famously a
Southsea resident, would certainly have endorsed
the sentiments. In heart at least, Southsea was a
place he never left:

With its imperial associations it is a glorious
place, and even now if I had to live in a town
outside London it is surely to Southsea, the
residential quarter of Portsmouth, that I
would return. The history of the past carries
into the history of today [...] There is a great
glamour there to anyone with the historic
sense – a sense which I drank in with my
mother's milk.

Clarence Esplanade

*Clarence Esplanade has a series of
monuments which in view of the heroic deeds
they recall would be difficult to match outside
Westminster Abbey or St Paul's Cathedral.*
GUIDE TO SOUTHSEA AND PORTSMOUTH
(WARD, LOCK, 1947)

Clarence Esplanade, which skirts the coast
between Clarence Pier and South Parade Pier,
offers a fascinating walk for those keen to explore
Portsmouth's rich maritime history. An array of
memorials reflects a city which has always looked
far beyond its own borders.

The largest and most impressive is the **Portsmouth
Naval Memorial** 'in honour of the Navy and to the
abiding memory of those ranks and ratings of this
port who laid down their lives in the defence of the

Empire and have no other grave than the sea.' Of the 24,588 men and women whose names are on the monument, 9,666 died during the First World War and 14,922 during the Second World War. The memorial adds: 'All were lost or buried at sea or were otherwise denied, by the fortunes of war, a known and honoured grave.'

Among the names is my great-uncle Bob Millener. He survived the sinking of HMS *Barham* in 1941 and was highly amused when my mother, just a child, accidentally bloodied his nose – something the Germans hadn't managed to do, he said. Sadly he died off the Normandy coast in the loss of HMS *Quorn*, a Hunt class destroyer, in 1944.

Behind the memorial stretches **Southsea Common**, one of Portsmouth's great open spaces and again a place rich in history. It was here that armies gathered before battle, perhaps most famously before the battle of Crécy. These days Southsea Common serves rather more peaceful purposes, such as picnicking, kite-flying or simply having a stroll. Thousands gathered on the Common in 2008 to watch Portsmouth's FA Cup final success played out live on a big screen; they returned the next day to watch manager Harry Redknapp and the team parade the cup through the city.

A number of other memorials are close by:

Sir Alec Rose (1908–1991) who 'landed on Southsea beach on 4th July 1968 on completion of his single-handed voyage round the world in *Lively Lady*.'

An anchor from HMS ***Victory*** on a stone plinth: 'Near this memorial on the 14th September 1805 Admiral Lord Nelson embarked for the last time, being killed on the following 21st October at the victorious Battle of Trafalgar.'

HMS *Trident*: 'To the memory of forty-four officers and men of HMS *Trident* who died of yellow fever in the short space of six weeks during the unusual epidemic at Sierra Leone 1859.'

Crimean War: 'Erected in memory of those brave soldiers and sailors who during the late war with Russia died of their wounds and are buried in this garrison.'

A little further back, by the Canoe Lake, is a memorial to the **Cockleshell Heroes**, unveiled on 6 July 1992, 'to mark the 50th Anniversary of this site which was used as a training base for the Royal Marine Boom Patrol Detachment formed on 6th July 1942. This secret unit trained on the Solent for raids by canoe (Cockles) on Europe. The most famous raid was on German shipping in Bordeaux docks on 11th December 1942 by ten members of RMBPD, only two of these Cockleshell Heroes returned.'

Southsea's Two Great Piers

Even if one of them isn't immediately obvious as such, Southsea is home to two piers, both a reflection of the changing nature of seaside entertainments down the decades.

One of only 55 private piers left in Britain, **South Parade Pier** was built in 1878 and has enjoyed a distinctly up-and-down history, falling victim to fire on three separate occasions. It had to be completely rebuilt after the first fire in 1904, and then rebuilt again after the second one in 1967. The third fire struck during the filming of The Who's rock opera *Tommy* on the pier in 1974.

Originally the pier was used as a terminal for ferries travelling to and from the Isle of Wight but soon it developed as a centre for entertainment. Seaside variety was the spice of its life, and its 1,200-seat theatre brought in the biggest names of the day. The *Southsea and Portsmouth Official Guide* of 1919 catches a flavour of its heyday when the pier staged 'a variety of events throughout the year including theatrical performances, vaudeville concert parties, military and other bands, carnival dances, aquatic sports and roller skating.'

It was requisitioned by the government during the Second World War and played a key role in the D-Day preparations and embarkation.

In November 2012 the pier was completely closed and fenced off by Portsmouth City Council as a danger to the public. The arcade, wholly on land at the head of the pier, was reopened, but the rest remains out of bounds, desperately in need of major investment. The bill for restoring it to anything approaching past glories is likely to be around £2 million. Its future is uncertain, to say the least.

The Clarence Pier is a very attractive building and includes an elegant concert hall with annexes for reading and other amusements.
CHARPENTIER'S PICTORIAL GUIDE TO SOUTHSEA
(1902)

Elegance and attractiveness are no longer the words which come to mind when you contemplate **Clarence Pier** today, but unlike South Parade Pier, at least it is still in use, lauded by its owners as 'one of the largest amusement parks on the south coast'. A more interesting distinction perhaps is the fact that rather than being at right-angles to the land in the conventional manner of piers, it doesn't so much point out to sea as hug the coast. It would be intriguing to know what the Victorians would make of it today.

The pier was opened in 1861 by the Prince and Princess of Wales and was originally known as Southsea Pier. Connected by tramline to Portsmouth

Town Railway Station (now Portsmouth & Southsea), the pier was at first another point of embarkation for the steam boats which connected Portsmouth and the Isle of Wight. The pier was badly damaged during the Second World War. It was rebuilt, and by the late 1950s it had gained its funfair. It can be seen, as can South Parade Pier, in the Mr Bean episode *Mind The Baby, Mr Bean*.

Telling the Story of Portsmouth

On the seafront Esplanade, half a mile or so to the east of South Parade Pier, is the **Royal Marines Museum**, another chance to explore the city's great military history. It opened in 1958 and tells the story of the Royal Marines from their beginnings in 1664 through to the present day.

The Museum is housed in the former Eastney Barracks which were originally constructed as the headquarters of the Royal Marine Artillery in the 1860s. My great-uncle Bert Millener (Bob's brother), who celebrated his 100th birthday in November 2012, joined the Royal Marines in 1929, trained at Deal and was sent to Eastney Barracks in 1931 before joining the aircraft carrier HMS *Courageous* the following September – one of many thousands of men to pass through Eastney.

One of the museum's highlights is its medal room with 8,000 medals on show.

A mile or so away, the story of the city of Portsmouth itself is told in another former barracks. **Portsmouth City Museum** in Museum Road explores the history of the city across a number of important collections: archaeology, art, Charles Dickens, local history, military history, natural science and oral history.

The Blitz

Portsmuthians are proud of this noble edifice,
and have good reason to be. Despite the
recent building of huge blocks and modern
offices, the Guildhall is still the most imposing
erection in the city.

SOUTHSEA AND THE CITY OF PORTSMOUTH
OFFICIAL GUIDE (1940)

Portsmouth was destined to be a target when
the Second World War came. The city's various
fortifications were a reflection of its strategic
importance; the Dockyard couldn't fail to interest
the Germans. In all, Portsmouth suffered sixty-seven
air raids. The first was in July 1940, the last in May
1944. A total of 930 civilians were killed, and more
than 1,200 badly injured. Around 6,000 houses were
destroyed; a similar number were badly damaged.

Among these, the highest-profile were the Guildhall and the Garrison Church.

Portsmouth's **Guildhall** today stands as both a memorial to the horrors of war and a symbol of the city's determination to move on. The building was virtually destroyed by German bombing in early 1941, but rose from its own ashes to become once again one of Portsmouth's most familiar landmarks.

We are bruised but we are not daunted, and we are still as determined as ever to stand side by side with other cities who have felt the blast of the enemy, and we shall, with them, persevere with an unflagging spirit towards a conclusive and decisive victory.

MAYOR OF PORTSMOUTH SIR DENIS DALEY WRITING IN THE CITY'S *EVENING NEWS*, 1941

Originally the Town Hall, it was designed in the neo-classical style by architect William Hill and built at a cost of £140,000 on land which had once been a brewery. Opened by the Prince and Princess of Wales (later Edward VII and Queen Alexandra) in 1890, it was conveniently near the new railway line now serving the growing city, and equipped with the latest amenities. The basement offered accommodation for the police station, the offices of the sanitary authority and the tramway committee. Above were the council chamber and the committee rooms. *Charpentier's Guide to Portsmouth and Southsea* (1913) tells us that the corridors and main hall were warmed with hot air. It doesn't mention whether it was the committee rooms which provided it.

The building's importance was underlined in 1926. With Portsmouth's elevation to city status, the Town Hall was renamed the Guildhall. Just fifteen years later, however, it was a smouldering wreck, gutted by some of the 40,000 incendiary bombs which fell on Portsmouth on the night of 10 January 1941. It was a night of thick cloud; only Portsmouth on the coast was easily recognisable, and it bore the brunt of the 153 bombers which attacked. Many bombs fell in the sea, but many did not.

The Guildhall famously took weeks to cool, but long before it did, it was obvious that it had effectively been destroyed. Most of the outer walls remained, but little else, and for many the only option was to demolish the ruin and start again. For others, however, demolition would have served to complete the Germans' work. So the remains were incorporated into the new building, which was opened by the Queen on 8 June 1959.

Today, the Guildhall serves as Portsmouth's biggest events venue, with a busy year-round programme including pop concerts, comedy and classical music. The building also hosts weddings, banquets, conferences and exhibitions.

It now looks out across a very different view to the one it used to enjoy, staring at its own reflection in the glass-fronted Civic Offices which now stand opposite. They were designed to complement the Guildhall, although some people would have preferred sufficient open space to step back and admire the Guildhall directly.

Opposite the Guildhall is a **statue of Queen Victoria**, the work of Alfred Dury. Standing on a square pedestal 17 feet high, the Queen is represented in imperial robes with sceptre and orb, ornamented by a figure of liberty. Erected by public subscription, the statue was unveiled on 8 July 1903, two and a half years after her death.

Nearby is another royal tribute, **Victoria √ Park**, which was opened in 1878, covering 15 acres of land granted to the Corporation by the War Department. It boasts conservatories, an aviary, rustic arbours and a fountain. It is also the location for a number of naval memorials. One of the entrances into Victoria Park, just next to the Guildhall, is through Portsmouth's First World War **Cenotaph**, guarded by statues of two gunners. The inscription reads:

This memorial was erected by the people of Portsmouth in proud and loving memory of those who in the glorious morning of their days for England's sake lost all but England's praise. May light perpetual shine upon them.

Nearby is the city's **Second World War memorial**, which bears the inscription:

In memory of the service men and women and the citizens of Portsmouth who gave their lives in defence of their country during World War II.

The night of 10 January 1941 was indeed a tragic one for Portsmouth. The same German raid which destroyed the Guildhall also gutted the **Garrison Church**, a scheduled ancient monument. Dating back to 1212–1220 when it was built as part of a hospital complex, the building had remained intact for more than seven centuries.

Originally part of the Hospital of St John and St Nicholas (*Domus Dei* or God's House), the church was closed under Henry VIII and briefly served as an armoury. Returning to a more fitting use, it was here that Charles II married Catherine of Braganza in 1662. Among other royal visits, George III and Queen Charlotte attended the Divine Service in 1778 at a time when the church held services for the troops of the garrison.

On the night of the 1941 bombing, the valiant efforts of the verger Mr J. Heaton, helped by assorted servicemen, saved the chancel. However, the flames swept through the nave which remains to this day roofless and open to the elements – a stark memorial to the men and women who gave their lives for their country.

Replacing the roof is no longer an option. Close to the sea, the exposed stonework has absorbed considerable amounts of salt solution over the years. If the roof were replaced, it seems the salt solution would crystallise and damage the walls. Consequently the building has been left as a partial ruin.

A particular point of interest is the large number of memorials the church contains, among them tributes to Horatio Nelson, the Duke of Wellington, and Lord Raglan, who lost an arm at Waterloo in 1815, but went on to command the British Army at the Crimea forty years later.

The night that destroyed the Guildhall and gutted the Garrison Church was one of the heaviest raids. Besides the thousands of incendiaries, the Luftwaffe also dropped 140 tons of high explosive bombs that night, killing 171 people and leaving 3,000 homeless. Clarence Pier, the Royal Hospital, Commercial Road, Kings Road, Palmerston Road and the Co-op department store in Fratton Road were just a few of the buildings and areas damaged. Also hit was Portsmouth and South Hampshire Eye and Ear Infirmary in Pembroke Road. Three cinemas, the Dockyard School and the Royal Sailors' Rest Home also suffered. Tragically the Arundel Street School air raid shelter suffered a direct hit, and 47 people died there alone on one of the grimmest nights in Portsmouth's history.

Houston Stewart Chamberlain (1855–1927) was born in Southsea, but had long since abandoned his homeland in favour of the Fatherland by the time of his death in Bayreuth. An ardent admirer of German culture and civilisation, arguably he helped lay the essential groundwork for the darkest decades the world has ever known with his virulent anti-Semitism and his total belief in the supremacy of the Aryan race. The rise of National Socialism and the murder of millions across Europe were the consequence of the kind of thinking Chamberlain passionately promoted. His most celebrated work was *The Foundations of the Nineteenth Century* (*Die Grundlagen des neunzehnten Jahrhunderts*, 1899), in which he wrote of the Germans as a positive force, the Jews as wholly negative. He acquired German citizenship during the First World War and used it to denounce vigorously the land of his birth. His views continued to gain momentum after his death. By the outbreak of the Second World War, *The Foundations* had sold a quarter of a million copies. Chamberlain is surely a son Portsmouth would prefer to forget.

PORTSMOUTH PEOPLE

Jailed for Witchcraft

Helen Duncan was the last person to be imprisoned under the British Witchcraft Act of 1735. Her crime was a séance in war-time Portsmouth.

Born in Scotland in 1897, Duncan made her living by conducting séances throughout the country. By 1941, she was living in Portsmouth, where, during one of her séances, a dead sailor apparently told her he had just gone down on HMS *Barham*, a vessel which was not officially declared lost until several weeks later.

Fearing disclosure of confidential information wherever it was coming from, the authorities began to take an interest in Duncan and the tales she was telling. In January 1944, one of her séances was raided and she was remanded in custody by Portsmouth magistrates. Duncan was accused of exploiting the bereaved, and she was sentenced to nine months in prison.

Lawyers stressed at the time that the purpose of the law was to root out belief in witchcraft rather than to punish witches. The distinction was an important one: Duncan was not convicted of being a witch. In the eyes of the law, her crime was to have claimed to possess the powers of a witch.

Hindsight seems to suggest the trial at the Old Bailey may have had something to do with the preparations for D-Day and a fear that Duncan might know or reveal something she shouldn't. Clearly security was the major concern. But the trial failed to impress Prime Minister Winston Churchill, as the 'Helen Duncan: the official pardon site' (www. helenduncan.org.uk) is pleased to point out. It cites Churchill's disdain for what was happening. He commented:

> *What was the cost of this trial to the State? – observing that witnesses were brought from Portsmouth and maintained here in this crowded London for a fortnight; and the Recorder kept busy with all this obsolete tomfoolery, to the detriment of necessary work in the courts.*

D-Day

On the central south coast, Portsmouth played a vital role in the planning and execution of **D-Day**, the largest amphibious invasion in history. The Normandy landings on 6 June 1944 significantly helped turn the tide against Hitler's Germany. In crossing the Channel to France, the vast air- and seaborne invasion force started the sweep which rolled the occupying German forces back to their homeland, signalling the end of the war.

The figures are staggering. On D-Day itself, the Allies landed around 156,000 troops in Normandy, supported by nearly 12,000 aircraft. The massive naval forces included very nearly 7,000 vessels. Five days later, nearly a third of a million men had reached the Normandy beaches, a monumental undertaking masterminded from Southwick House, just north of Portsmouth. In the months leading up to D-Day, the house served as headquarters for the main Allied commanders including Allied Supreme Commander General Eisenhower, Army Commander-in-Chief General Montgomery and the Naval Commander-in-Chief Admiral Ramsay. As D-Day approached, the area around Portsmouth became a huge holding bay for troops and armoured vehicles waiting for the off; the view from Portsmouth's Round Tower must have been impressive indeed as countless ships awaited their orders. And then just as suddenly they were gone.

Operation Neptune was the landing; Operation Overlord was the Battle of Normandy which ensued, opening the way for the invasion of German-occupied western Europe. It's a story told in the **D-Day Museum** in Southsea which was opened by Queen Elizabeth, The Queen Mother in June 1984, on the fortieth anniversary of D-Day. The museum's centrepiece is the Overlord Embroidery, at 83 metres the longest embroidery of its kind in the world. The Bayeux Tapestry commemorated the Norman invasion of England; the Overlord Embroidery celebrates the Allied invasion of Normandy.

PORTSMOUTH CULTURE

The Goon who Gave us Clouseau

Arguably the greatest acting son of Portsmouth is the man who starred in *The Goons* and as hapless Chief Inspector Clouseau in *The Pink Panther* series of films. On 96 Castle Road, Southsea, an English Heritage blue plaque reads simply '**Peter Sellers** 1925–1980 Actor and Comedian was born here.' 'Born into show business', it might have added. Sellers was the only child of vaudeville performers William Sellers and Agnes (Peg) Marks who were appearing in Southsea when Peter arrived. At the age of two weeks, their baby followed in their footsteps, making his stage debut at the Kings Theatre.

Sellers, real name Richard Henry Sellers, was educated in London, leaving school at fourteen. Initially, he seemed destined for a career as a jazz drummer, but the war intervened. Sellers joined the RAF and ended up in its entertainment section in India, Ceylon and Burma with Ralph Reader's gang show. After the war, he made his way in radio shows, culminating in *The Goon Show* which ran for nine years from 1951, co-starring Spike Milligan, Harry Secombe and Michael Bentine.

Sellers' big film break was *The Ladykillers* (1955), but probably his biggest impact was as Inspector Clouseau in *The Pink Panther* (1963), *A Shot in the Dark* (1964), *The Return of the Pink Panther* (1975) and *The Pink Panther Strikes Again* (1976). Sellers died, aged 54, in the Middlesex Hospital, London, on 24 July 1980 following a heart attack. Fellow actor Richard Attenborough commented that Sellers 'had the genius comparable to Chaplin'.

Sellers' fellow Goon Spike Milligan famously nominated Portsmouth to be put into Room 101 in an edition of the TV show first broadcast on BBC Two on 5 August 1999. His reason? Because he appeared on stage there three times 'and I died the bloody death!' It was initially disallowed by host Paul Merton because 'if Portsmouth wasn't there, the south coast would fray at the edges', but Merton then acquiesced after the audience's reaction to Milligan's disappointment. Named after the torture room in the novel *Nineteen Eighty-Four* by George Orwell, Room 101 is offered in the show as a fate worse than death.

PORTSMOUTH TIMES

Post-War Development

For centuries, packed on its Portsea Island home, Portsmouth was a byword for overcrowding – a social ill which the city's great nineteenth-century humanitarians did much to highlight. However, it wasn't until the aftermath of war in the middle of the twentieth century that serious, indeed radical, efforts were made to tackle the problem. With its rising population and dangerously high inner-city densities, the post-war city simply had to grow in the only direction it could: northwards.

Portsmouth began planning before the war had ended. In 1944, around 2,000 acres were acquired at Leigh Park on a site which Portsmouth Council was determined to develop as the Garden City of the South. Building work began after the war, and in 1949 the first residents moved in. Cities up and down the country were doing exactly the same, offering cramped and crowded inner-city inhabitants the chance of a better life at the other end of a short trip out into the countryside. Wecock Farm and Crookhorn were other new estates – and Portsmouth achieved its aim. The city itself saw its population drop from very nearly a quarter of a million people in 1931 to just under 200,000 by the end of the 1960s, falling still further to 177,142 in 1991. Meanwhile to the north, Bedhampton, Cosham, Drayton, Horndean, Havant, Portchester, Waterlooville, Widley and Wymering Garden City all grew significantly. Within the city, the retraction of defence establishments released land for housing at sites including Gunwharf and Eastney Barracks.

Portsmouth's lost hospitals

The Royal Hospital, founded in 1847 on a site off Commercial Road now occupied by Sainsbury's, closed in 1978, and its activities were transferred to the Queen Alexandra Hospital – QA – at Cosham, just north of the city centre. Famously the Royal once housed a 'lock ward' for the compulsory treatment of prostitutes under the provisions of the Contagious Diseases Acts, in force from 1864 until their repeal in 1886.

The Portsmouth and South Hampshire Eye and Ear Infirmary, destroyed by German bombs on 10 January 1941, was relocated to Grove Road North where I and thousands of other visually challenged children of the 1960s well remember endlessly lining up cartoon characters as the staff attempted to assess the shortcomings of our eyesight. It closed in 1971 and its functions transferred to QA.

PORTSMOUTH PLACES

'A mildewed lump of elephant droppings'

If it wasn't actually the ugliest building in the UK, it was certainly a strong contender, and yet Portsmouth's Tricorn Centre, which opened in 1966, wasn't without its fans when it was finally demolished.

Described by Prince Charles as 'a mildewed lump of elephant droppings', the Tricorn Centre was for many years the city's best-known eyesore, brutalist architecture at its best or worst, depending on your point of view.

Originally designed to revitalise Portsmouth, it consisted of a shopping centre, complete with market area, night club, pub and multi-storey car park. It was created by Owen Luder and Rodney Gordon in the tricorn shape which gave it its name.

In the 1980s, Portsmouth's Tricorn Centre was voted the third ugliest building in the UK, a distinction it topped when BBC Radio 4 listeners decided it was the UK's most hated building in 2001. Three years later, Heritage Minister Andrew McIntosh decided it was not worth listing, a move hailed by Portsmouth City Council as a 'great day for Portsmouth' – much to the dismay of Owen Luder:

> It's a great pity that it will not be listed. It is a 'gee whiz' building, not a 'so what' building.
> THE GUARDIAN (10 MARCH 2004)

Demolition began that very month. The site is now largely a car park, serving Portsmouth's Cascades Shopping Centre.

Education, Education, Education

John Relly Beard (1800–1876) saw lack of education as the principal source of society's ills, and he promoted it with full Unitarian fervour. Born at 24 Charlotte Row, Landport, Portsmouth, he was educated in the city before preparing for the ministry at Manchester College in York. Seeing all that was lacking in the education provision, he took the authorities to task with his *The Abuses of the Manchester Free Grammar School* (1837), which paved the way for important reforms. He followed it up with widely regarded textbooks including his *Dictionary of the Bible* and *Latin Made Easy*. However, many regard his finest achievement as his part in the creation of the Unitarian Home Missionary Board in 1854 for the training of young men for home missions. He served as principal. The establishment eventually became part of the University of Manchester.

The son of a Portsea vicar, **William Macbride Childs** (1869–1939) was educated at Portsmouth Grammar School and accepted a lectureship in history at the University of Oxford's extension college in Reading, rising to become its principal. The college became Reading University College in 1902, but Childs' ambition was to turn it into a full university in its own right, despite lack of money and proximity to Oxford. Childs relished it all as an adventure, which he chronicled in *Making a University: an Account of the University Movement at Reading* (1933). When the University of Reading received its charter in 1926, Childs became the first vice-chancellor.

The sudden death of **Dame Judith Kilpatrick** robbed Portsmouth of a towering figure in the field of education. Dame Judith (1952–2002) was directing a teacher-training session when she collapsed and died, aged 50. Her obituary in *The Guardian* described her as 'an inspirational headteacher and educational powerhouse with a huge capacity for work.'

Her impact had spread far beyond the successful City of Portsmouth Girls' School she had run for the last seven years. In 1998 the Office for Standards in Education praised her superb leadership. Kilpatrick was appointed a dame in 2000, only the second teacher to be thus honoured, and her reaction summed up her philosophy:

It reflects well on all my colleagues, and that's the important thing... Schools are about partnerships. It's about trusting your staff. Setting the parameters against which we're going to work, but then trusting people to do that – monitoring, supporting, and generally working with colleagues not above colleagues.

On her death, one of the tributes left at the school read simply:

You made this school bloom, and even though you are no longer here, it will continue to bloom because of you.

PORTSMOUTH CULTURE

Play Up, Pompey!

It's a favourite question for every fan of **Portsmouth Football Club**: which club has held the FA Cup longer than any other football team? The answer is, of course, Portsmouth, helped by the fact that they won it in 1939 and the competition was then suspended at the outbreak of war.

When the competition was next contested, Derby County became the first post-war victors. But Pompey's 1939 victory – 4–1 against Wolverhampton Wanderers in front of very nearly 100,000 people at the original Wembley Stadium – was the stuff of Portsmouth dreams. The dreams lived again sixty-nine years later when manager Harry Redknapp took them all the way to the final, this time for a 1–0 victory against Cardiff City in the new Wembley stadium. The next day the team – watched by tens of thousands of cheering fans – paraded the trophy around the streets of Portsmouth on a triumphant open-top bus tour.

The victory was to be the highlight of Pompey's spell in football's Premiership. They arrived there in 2003 and were relegated to the Championship in 2010. Relegation from the Championship to League One followed at the end of the 2011–2012 season – all against a background of massive debts and a grim financial crisis which put the club's very future in doubt. Still, the club managed to inspire in its fans a passionate loyalty which is the envy of higher-flying teams up and down the country.

This loyalty found its greatest expression on a landmark day in April 2013 when the Pompey Supporters Trust took the club into community ownership, making it the largest fan-owned football club in English football history. The 2012–2013 season ended with Portsmouth's relegation to League Two, the fourth tier of English football, but the Trust deal means that – despite the relegation – the much-troubled club will start the 2013–2014 season with renewed optimism and a great sense of a new beginning.

The club was founded in 1898 and joined the Southern League in 1899. Its home has always been Fratton Park, a place where the glory days have included successive league titles in 1948–1949 and 1949–1950, at a time when the club benefitted from having the pick of the former professional footballers who stayed in the area after serving in the Dockyard during the Second World War.

Portsmouth's first kit was a salmon pink shirt with white shorts and maroon socks. In 1909 they changed to white shirts with royal blue shorts and socks, then again two years later to blue shirts, white shorts and black socks. The black socks were later switched to red.

PORTSMOUTH CULTURE

Portsmouth's Musicians

Joseph Reinagle (1762–1825) was an instrumentalist and composer born in Portsmouth, the son of an Austrian trumpeter. Reinagle played cello at the Handel Commemoration in Westminster Abbey in 1784, an event marking the twenty-fifth anniversary of Handel's death. After a stint in Dublin, Reinagle returned to London where he received encouragement and advice as a composer from Haydn. He composed a considerable amount of music for violin and cello, particularly duets, but much of his work has been lost. Reinagle also wrote *A Concise Introduction to the Art of Playing the Violoncello* (*c.*1800).

The Victorian harpist **John Balsir Chatterton** (1804–1871) was born in Portsmouth. He studied the harp in London and became a professor at the Royal Academy of Music in 1827. A prolific composer, he was appointed harpist to the Queen in 1842.

Those august Victorian gentlemen, Messrs **Gilbert & Sullivan** set their comic opera HMS *Pinafore, or The Lass that loved a Sailor* (1878) on board a ship in Portsmouth. Also set in the docks at Portsmouth is the Gilbert & Sullivan-inspired one-act comic ballet *Pineapple Poll*, which premiered in 1951, with choreography and libretto by Cranko, music by Arthur Sullivan (arranged by Charles Mackerras) and designs by Osbert Lancaster.

Portsmouth Point, or Spice Island, was always one of the more colourful parts of Old Portsmouth, named after the area's involvement in the trade of Caribbean spices. Its reputation also rested on the pubs, brothels and generally lewd behaviour to be found there – aspects captured in **Thomas Rowlandson**'s etching *Portsmouth Point* (1800). The etching in turn inspired **Sir William Walton**'s overture for orchestra of the same name, composed in 1925.

Southsea-born **David Heneker** (1906–2001) was the man commissioned to turn H. G. Wells' *Kipps* into a stage musical for rock star Tommy Steele. The result was *Half a Sixpence* (1963). Heneker's first hit was *There Goes My Dream* in 1940. After service in Tunisia during the Second World War, he became the pianist at the Embassy Club in London's Bond Street in the 1950s. Collaborations included *Expresso Bongo* and *Irma La Douce* (both 1958).

The jazz musician, bandleader, entertainer, drummer, guitarist, pianist, songwriter and singer **Cab Kaye**, also **Quaye** (1921–2000), was born of an

English mother and Gold Coast father in London but brought up in Portsmouth. Real name Augustus Nii-Lante Kwamlah Quaye, he auditioned at the age of 14 for bandleader Billy Cotton with whom he toured and sang. After the war, he made his name among the new wave of jazz modernists. His *Ministers of Swing* included the leading jazz modernists Ronnie Scott and John Dankworth. Kaye reached his largest audience in 1958 through the television programme *6–5 Special*. He died from cancer in Amsterdam on 13 March 2000.

Born George W. Lowen Coxhill in Portsmouth in 1932, **Lol Coxhill** was a free-improvising saxophonist and raconteur who toured the US air bases after the war and played with visiting American musicians in the 1960s. He worked in a number of small collaborative groups and also worked with musicians including Mike Oldfield, The Damned and Hugh Metcalfe. He died on 9 July 2012.

Simon Dupree and the Big Sound were a British psychedelic rock band formed by three brothers, **Derek Shulman** (*b.* 1947), **Phil Shulman** (*b.* 1937), and **Ray Shulman** (*b.* 1949). Derek and Phil were born in Glasgow, but Ray was born in Portsmouth, and it was in the Portsmouth area that they started playing, first as The Howling Wolves and then The Road Runners before becoming Simon Dupree and the Big Sound in 1966. They later became the progressive rock group Gentle Giant.

Manfred Mann and Blues Band star, Gospel singer and broadcaster **Paul Jones** is a Portsmouth man, born Paul Pond in the city on 24 February 1942. Brian Jones invited him to join the band which became The Rolling Stones, but Paul declined. He made his name instead with the Mann Hugg Blues Brothers which became Manfred Mann. Hits included '5-4-3-2-1', 'Do Wah Diddy Diddy' and 'Pretty Flamingo' before Jones left the line-up to go solo in 1966. He recently featured on the band's fiftieth anniversary tour. He has a busy broadcasting schedule, hosting weekly blues and gospel radio programmes.

Five-times Grammy Award-nominated singer-songwriter **Joe Jackson** (*b.* 11 August 1954) grew up in the Paulsgrove area of Portsmouth and attended the City of Portsmouth Boys' School. Jackson was signed to A&M Records in the summer of 1978 and made his debut with 'Is She Really Going Out With Him?' which remains one of his best-known songs. The albums *Look Sharp!*, *I'm The Man* and *Beat Crazy* were released between 1979 and 1980. The single 'It's Different for Girls' reached number five. Studio and live albums have followed ever since including *The Duke* in 2012, his unconventional salute to Duke Ellington.

Born in Portsmouth on 22 August 1961, **Roland Orzabal** (real name Roland Jaime Orzabal de la Quintana) is a musician, songwriter and record producer best known as one of the co-founders, with Curt Smith, of Tears for Fears. Their song 'Everybody Wants to Rule the World' won the Brit

Award for Best British Single in 1986. Other hits included 'Mad World', 'Shout' and 'Sowing the Seeds of Love'. The band has sold more than 25 million albums worldwide.

Julia Fordham, born in Portsmouth on 10 August 1962, was one of Mari Wilson's backing vocalists, the Wilsations, before setting out a on a solo career, achieving chart success with 'Happy Ever After' in 1988. Her debut album *Julia Fordham* (1988) reached the top 20. Further success came with *(Love Moves In) Mysterious Ways* in 1992. *The Julia Fordham Collection* was released in 1998, followed by *Unusual Suspects*, a collaboration with Paul Reiser. The album *Under the Rainbow* was released in July 2013.

Run, Portsmouth, Run!

Flat and conducive to speed with its wide roads and promenade, Portsmouth is an ideal place to run. Not surprisingly it has spawned two great and appealingly different races.

The Great South Run is a ten-mile race every October, starting from Southsea seafront, taking in Old Portsmouth and the Dockyard before heading out towards Eastney, then turning for a bracing promenade run back to the start. Launched in 1990, it was originally held in Southampton before moving to Portsmouth where it proclaims itself as 'the world's premier ten-mile running event', run by

25,000 people a year. The list of winners over the years is a Who's Who of running: Paula Radcliffe, the world's fastest-ever woman marathon-runner, won the women's race in 2008; the following year, Mo Farah won it for the men – before going on to win two golds at the 2012 London Olympics.

For those who prefer a full marathon, the **Portsmouth Coastal Waterside Marathon**, which was run for the first time in 2010, has rapidly acquired a glowing reputation as an invigorating race along an outstandingly different course – around three sides of Langstone Harbour to the end of the former Hayling Billy railway line and back, just a few days before Christmas. One of the great incentives for keeping on going is that you might just get your feet wet if you don't.

Olympic athlete **Alan Pascoe** was born in Portsmouth on 11 October 1947. Pascoe won silver in the 4×400 metre relay at the 1972 Olympic Games and also secured medals in the European Championships and the Commonwealth Games.

PORTSMOUTH PEOPLE

A Unique Achievement in Politics

Too full of drugs, obesity, underachievement and Labour MPs.

<small>FORMER CONSERVATIVE MP AND CURRENT MAYOR OF LONDON BORIS JOHNSON ON THE CITY OF PORTSMOUTH (2007)</small>

James Callaghan (1912–2005) is the only politician√ in history to have served in all four of the Great Offices of State, having been Chancellor of the Exchequer from 1964 to 1967, Home Secretary from 1967 to 1970, Foreign Secretary from 1974 to 1976 and Prime Minister from 1976 to 1979 – a remarkable achievement for a man Portsmouth can call its own. Callaghan was elevated to the Lords as Baron Callaghan of Cardiff, the city for which he served as MP, but it was in Portsmouth that he was born, at 38 Funtington Road, Copnor, on 27 March 1912, the only son of Petty Officer James Callaghan. Callaghan's father became a coastguard at Brixham after the First World War, but when he died suddenly of a heart attack (James was nine at the time), the family moved back to Portsmouth where they lived at a number of different addresses. Callaghan attended Portsmouth Northern Secondary School, but the greater influence was the Baptist church which kept a paternal eye on him when he became a clerk with the Inland Revenue at the age of seventeen in their Maidstone office. He entered Parliament in 1945 and succeeded Harold Wilson as Prime Minister in 1976.

Gunwharf

Today, **Gunwharf Quays**, with its beautiful harbourside location, is one of the great Portsmouth attractions, home to around a hundred shops, dozens of restaurants, a multi-screen cinema, night clubs and comedy clubs, a bowling alley and attractive accommodation, all crowned by the elegant Spinnaker Tower towering above them.

Gunwharf Quays is a place which positively buzzes with life, comfortably one of the most successful transformation schemes in the city's recent history. Dotted around it are reminders – moorings and figureheads – of the site's more distant past which lives on in its name. Situated just to the south of the Dockyard, Gunwharf Quays was the site of the navy's arsenal. Here weapons and ammunition would be taken from ships as they arrived in the harbour and ships would be resupplied as they headed back out to sea.

The *Victoria County History* paints a vivid picture of how it must have been in its naval heyday:

> *Near the Camber is a dry dock for trading vessels, and still farther north is the Gun Wharf, the arsenal where is stored ordnance both for the fleet and for the garrison of the town. It consists of the old and the new Gun Wharf, separated by a small basin where barges enter to carry the naval guns from the wharf to the battleships in the dockyard, or to unlade stores of rifles and bayonets, which are kept in the Armoury. The latter is ingeniously decorated with obsolete weapons and armour of all descriptions and from all countries. The main entrance of the wharf is near the United Service Recreation Grounds, which form a fine open space between Portsea and Portsmouth.*
>
> *A HISTORY OF THE COUNTY OF HAMPSHIRE: VOLUME 3 (1908)*

The *Southsea and Portsmouth Official Guide* (1919) described it as home to 'the finest collection of weapons outside the Tower of London, including more than 25,000 rifles'. The site was severely damaged during the Second World War, with many notable buildings razed to the ground. After the war, it became Royal Navy shore establishment HMS *Vernon* before its redevelopment as the shopping centre, which opened in 2001.

PORTSMOUTH CULTURE

Stage and Screen

John Bernard (1756–1828) was born in Portsmouth and lived the life of a strolling player of his day. He worked extensively in Britain in the first half of his career, managing theatres in Plymouth, Brighton and Guernsey, and in North America in the second, as an actor and actor-manager in Boston, New York, Montreal and Quebec City.

Hailed as 'the most beloved of 19th century Boston actresses' in *The Oxford Companion to American Theatre,* **Mrs J. R. Vincent** (1818–1887), née Mary Ann Farley, was born in Portsmouth and made her debut in Cowes in 1835. She and her husband, the comedian James R. Vincent, played Boston's National Theatre in 1846 and she remained in the city after his death. Vincent appeared in a remarkable 444 plays at the Boston Museum theatre in roles including Portia, Gertrude, Mrs Malaprop, Lady Teazle and Nancy Sykes.

Theatre manager and playwright **James William Whitbread** (1847–1916) was born in Portsmouth, a supporting actor who managed and wrote for the Queen's Theatre, Dublin, which he transformed through his leadership. His works included *Lord Edward Fitzgerald* (1894), *Theobald Wolfe Tone* (1898), *The Ulster Hero* (1902), *The Insurgent Chief* (1902) and *The Sham Squire* (1903).

Rosalinde Fuller (1901–1982) was another Portsmouth-born English actress who enjoyed success in America where she played Ophelia to John Barrymore's Hamlet in 1922. Her principal work was in this country, however, notably with Donald Wolfit's Shakespeare company from 1938 to 1940, years which saw her play many of Shakespeare's heroines. Fuller later specialised in her own solo programmes consisting of her own adaptations of short sketches from authors including Dickens, Maupassant and Henry James.

As unlikely as it sounds, Portsmouth can claim literally to have helped shape the hard-man actor and former Governor of California **Arnold Schwarzenegger** (*b.* 30 July 1947). In 1966, aged 19 and just out of national service with the Austrian army, Schwarzenegger came to London to compete in the Mr Universe competition. There he met Wag Bennett, owner of a gym in London's Forest Gate. Schwarzenegger came second in the competition, after which Wag and his wife Dianne introduced themselves – the start of a warm friendship, so warm in fact that Schwarzenegger came to regard the Bennetts as his British parents. Today Dianne runs the same gym in Portsmouth her father once owned. Schwarzenegger often came to stay and remains a close friend.

John Madden, born in Portsmouth on 8 April 1949, has directed a string of acclaimed films including *Mrs Brown* (1997), *Shakespeare in Love* (1998), *Captain Corelli's Mandolin* (2001), *Proof* (2005), *The Debt* (2011) and *The Best Exotic Marigold Hotel* (2012). Judi Dench and Gwyneth Paltrow have both won Oscars in his movies. Madden's small-screen credits include *Sherlock Holmes*, several episodes of *Inspector Morse* and the TV movie *Truth or Dare*.

Olivier Award-nominated actress, singer and comedian **Dillie Keane** (*b.* 23 May 1952) was brought up in Portsmouth and retains a strong affection for the city. She is an enthusiastic and supportive patron of the Kings Theatre. Keane is best known as one-third of the cabaret trio *Fascinating Aïda* which she founded in 1983, but she has also had a prominent solo career.

Portsmouth Football Club fanatic and Oscar-winning director **Anthony Minghella** (1954–2008) was educated in Portsmouth. The son of a famous family of Isle of Wight ice cream factory owners, he attended St John's College in Southsea. Minghella won the Academy Award for Best Director for *The English Patient* in 1996. His tragic death from a haemorrhage at the age of 54 followed cancer surgery. He remained a life-long Pompey supporter with an extensive collection of club memorabilia.

Film producer **Alison Owen**, whose credits include *Elizabeth* (1998), *Sylvia* (2003), *Shaun of the Dead* (2004), *Proof* (2005) and *The Other Boleyn Girl* (2007), was born in Portsmouth in 1961 and educated in the city. Her son Alfie Allen was born in London, but attended St John's College in Southsea. Her daughter is the pop star Lily Allen.

Preachers and Priests

Portsmouth has a long tradition of being an inspiration to preachers and priests.

Former slave and preacher **John Jea** (*b. c.*1773; *d.* after 1817) chronicled his adventures in *The Life, History, and Unparalleled Sufferings of John Jea, the African Preacher.* Born in Africa, he spent his childhood in New York where he was taken into slavery at the age of two and a half, along with his family. Jea claimed he used the fact of his Christian baptism to compel his master to set him free, after which he preached widely in North America and Europe. Some of his tales seem just a little tall now, such as being granted the ability to read the Bible and nothing else in answer to a prayer, but there is no doubting the energy of his evangelism which eventually carried him across the Atlantic to England where a more receptive audience prompted him to preach with renewed vigour. He found particular success in Ireland, marrying an Irishwoman with whom he settled in Portsmouth.

In his early years, **Thomas Shillitoe** (1754–1836), was apprenticed to a grocer and worked for a time in Portsmouth, but his calling lay elsewhere. He was able to retire from business in the early years of the nineteenth century to concentrate on his Quaker and philanthropic interests, for which he travelled widely on both sides of the Atlantic, challenging drinkers to mend their ways.

Roman Catholic nun, **Mary Cecilia Potter** (1847–1913) was educated in London and moved to Southsea where she ran a small school before

becoming convinced that her real calling was to
establish a new order of Catholic Sisters dedicated
to the care of the dying. The idea met with strong
opposition, not least because she was often seen as
rather unstable. She persisted, however, and with
the backing of the Bishop of Nottingham launched
the Little Company of Mary in a disused factory in
Nottinghamshire. Her work gained the support of
Pope Leo XIII who invited her to set up a hospital
for the English community in Rome – a hospital
which became the first Italian school for professional
nurses. As her success grew, so Potter sent sisters
from the Little Company of Mary further afield,
setting up communities in Australia, Ireland, the
United States, Malta and South Africa. Potter was
declared venerable by Pope John Paul II in 1988, a
step towards possible canonisation.

Certainly not a title to delight the city's tourism
bosses, *Ten Years in a Portsmouth Slum* (1896) was an
important document in late Victorian Portsmouth,
the work of Robert William Radclyffe Dolling, better
known as **Father Dolling** (1851–1902). An Irishman
by birth, he was educated at Harrow and Trinity

College, Cambridge and worked initially in London before being put in charge of St Agatha's, Landport, Portsmouth. It was here that he wrought the transformation he chronicled in his book, battling vigorously against the squalor he found: destitution, drunkenness and prostitution were his enemies, and, as he looked back in the opening lines of his memoir, he knew the progress he had made:

> *I fear the title of this little book is almost a libel; but, as the parent often looks upon the grown-up son as if he were still a child, so do my thoughts ever go back to the infancy of our work, and S. Agatha's is a slum district in my mind. Though we have largely lost the outward visible signs of slumdom, poverty, of course, remains – it always will – but utter hopelessness and callous depravity have, in a measure, passed away, not merely from our people, but from our very streets.*

Cyril Forster Garbett (1875–1955) was born in Surrey and sent to board at Portsmouth Grammar

School in 1886. After studying at Oxford and training for ordination at Cuddesdon Theological College, he became curate in 1900 at St Mary, Portsea, at the time a huge Dockyard parish. Garbett, who progressed from curate to vicar, saw the effects of alcohol in his parish and took the local brewers to task. His connection with Portsmouth ended in 1919 when he was appointed Bishop of Southwark, where he campaigned for the new housing estates of south London and determinedly set up new churches. He became Bishop of Winchester in 1932 and Archbishop of York in 1942.

Derek Worlock (1920–1996), most famously Roman Catholic Archbishop of Liverpool, was earlier the sixth Bishop of Portsmouth. Appointed on 18 October 1965, Worlock held the post for ten years, during which time he was appointed episcopal secretary of the Catholic Bishops' Conference of England and Wales. He was also an active member of the international Synod of Bishops.

Cardinal Cormac Murphy-O'Connor was appointed the tenth Archbishop of Westminster – and therefore head of the Catholic Church in England and Wales – on 15 February 2000. Born on 24 August 1932 in Reading, he was ordained in 1956 and served in parishes in Portsmouth and Fareham before becoming director of vocations for the diocese of Portsmouth. In 1966 Murphy-O'Connor was appointed private secretary and chaplain to the newly appointed Roman Catholic Bishop of Portsmouth, Derek Worlock, and in 1971 was appointed rector of the English College in Rome. Murphy-O'Connor returned to the UK after being appointed Bishop of Arundel and Brighton in 1977.

PORTSMOUTH PLACES

Centres of Learning

The University of Portsmouth bills itself as 'a university by the sea but in the heart of one of Britain's most historic cities'. It is also the top modern university in the United Kingdom in the *Times Higher Education* World University Rankings, with a reputation that rests on teaching and research. Many of its academics are international leaders in their fields. Its 23,000-plus students are supported by more than 2,500 staff. The university was founded as the Portsmouth and Gosport School of Science and the Arts in 1869, strongly linked to Portsmouth Dockyard for which it trained engineers and skilled workmen. With the decline of the Dockyard, however, the college was forced to diversify the subjects it taught, becoming Portsmouth Polytechnic as part of the massive expansion in higher education in the 1960s. Its next step forward came in 1992

when, along with other polytechnics, it was granted
university status.

For ten years **Malcolm Fewtrell** (1909–2005) was accommodation officer for Portsmouth Polytechnic before retiring to a bungalow in Swanage, Dorset. It was a quiet end to a distinguished career for the police officer charged with solving the Great Train Robbery.

Detective Superintendent Fewtrell, head of Buckinghamshire CID, was less than a year away from retirement when the crime of the century tumbled into his lap. At about 4.30 a.m. on 8 August 1963, police HQ in Aylesbury phoned him with the message: 'There's been a train robbery at Cheddington, sir.' The Glasgow to London mail had been robbed; nearly £2.6 million had been taken; and it was Fewtrell who correctly guessed that the gang would be holed up nearby. His account, *The Train Robbers*, was published in 1964.

Another centre of learning, with a rather longer history, is **Portsmouth Grammar School** which was founded in 1732 under the terms of the will of William Smith, a former Mayor of Portsmouth and garrison physician. It has gone on to become one of the top public schools in the UK.

Former pupils of Portsmouth Grammar School are known as Old Portmuthians. Among them was one of the world's greatest ever batsmen. Cricketer **Wally Hammond** (1903–1965) was born at the Royal Garrison at Dover Castle, the only child of Corporal (later Major) William Walter Hammond. His father's postings meant that young Wally spent his earliest years in China and Malta, but when the First World

War broke out, he was sent to Portsmouth Grammar School. Hammond went on to score a remarkable 50,551 runs at an average of 56.10 in a dazzling cricketing career. Thirty-six of his 167 centuries were doubles. He scored twenty-two centuries for England, with a highest score of 336 not out, among 7,249 Test runs at an average of 58.45.

Other Old Portmuthians include author Percy F. Westerman (1876–1959), novelist James Clavell (1924–1994), poet Christopher Logue (1926–2011), singer Paul Jones (*b.* 1942) and athlete Roger Black (*b.* 1966).

Portsmouth is also home to **St John's College**, an independent Catholic day and boarding school in Southsea, founded by the De La Salle brothers who run it still. It was established in 1908, moving to its present site in 1914.

Other Portsmouth secondary schools are Admiral Lord Nelson School, Charter Academy, the City of Portsmouth Girls' School, King Richard School, Mayfield School, Miltoncross School, Priory School, Springfield School, St Edmund's Catholic School and the City of Portsmouth Boys' School.

Portsmouth's Modern Writers

Children's author **Percy Francis Westerman** (1876–1959) was one of the most prolific writers of his generation and considered the best adventure writer of his day, producing scores of books, mostly with a military theme. Westerman was born at 41 Kensington Terrace, Portsea and educated at Portsmouth Grammar School. His first book was *A Lad of Grit,* published in 1908; a couple of years later, he turned to writing full-time. His output was substantial.

Richard Aldington (born Edward Godfree Aldington) was an established poet by the time of the outbreak of the First World War, in which he was determined to serve. He survived the trenches and in 1919 published the collection *War and Love*. He worked extensively as a critic and translator, combining in the two his love of France. Towards the end of the 1920s, he abandoned poetry in favour of the novel. His first, the anti-war *Death of a Hero* (1929), was the turning point which made his name. He later moved to the States and worked as a screenwriter in Hollywood for much of the Second World War. Later works included his biography of Lawrence, *D. H. Lawrence: Portrait of a Genius, but ...* (1950). More controversial was his treatment of another Lawrence in *Lawrence of Arabia: a Biographical Enquiry* (1955) in which he attacked the T. E. Lawrence legend. Aldington was born in 1892 at 50 High Street, Portsmouth and died in 1962. His legacy for the city is a poem which includes the lines, 'I hate that town; I hate the town I lived in when I was little; I hate to think of it.' 'Childhood' continues in similar vein across more than 120 lines.

Novelist and aeronautical engineer **Nevil Shute** (1899–1960) lived in the Portsmouth area –

including two addresses in Southsea – from 1933 until he moved to Australia in 1950. His novels include *Pied Piper* (1942), *A Town Like Alice* (1950) and *On the Beach* (1957). A number of locations in and around the city are mentioned in his novels. He also founded the Airspeed company at Portsmouth airport; Nevil Shute Road and Airspeed Road were named in his honour.

Portsmouth-born journalist and writer **Olivia Manning** (1908–1980) put her life and times into her novels. It is with her *Balkan Trilogy* (*The Great Fortune*, 1960; *The Spoilt City*, 1962; *Friends and Heroes*, 1965) that her reputation principally rests. She also wrote *The Levant Trilogy* (*The Danger Tree*, 1977; *The Battle Lost and Won*, 1978; *The Sum of Things*, 1980). The two trilogies are considered an important literary response to the Second World War. She was born at 134 Laburnum Grove, North End, Portsmouth.

Robert Gittings (1911–1992) is best known for his literary biographies, *John Keats* (1969), *The Young Thomas Hardy* (1975) and *The Older Hardy* (1978), though he also wrote a number of collections of poetry. The son of a naval surgeon, he was born in Southsea.

Shogun author **James Clavell** was born the son of a British Royal Navy captain in Sydney, Australia, in 1921 and died a naturalised American in 1994, but it was in Portsmouth that he grew up. Real name Charles Edmund Dumaresq Clavell, he attended Portsmouth Grammar School, joined the Royal Artillery in 1940 and was sent to Singapore where he was captured by the Japanese in 1941. Clavell endured four years in the notorious Changi camp where very few survived. He later claimed that this was the university he never had. Clavell emigrated to New York in 1953, moving to Los Angeles a year later where he became a screenwriter. His films included *The Fly* and *Watusi* (both 1958). He also worked on *633 Squadron* (1963), *The Great Escape* (1966) and *To Sir, with Love* (1966). His novels include *King Rat* (1962), *Tai Pan* (1966) and his most popular, *Shogun* (1975).

The poet, playwright and translator **Christopher Logue** (1926–2011) was born and educated in Portsmouth. After serving with the British army towards the end of the Second World War, he moved to France and then London. For many years he edited the 'True Stories' column for *Private Eye*. He was keen to bring poetry closer to popular experience, and produced a number of Poster Poems in the 1960s as part of the jazz poetry movement. Among his collections are *Ode to the Dodo: Poems from 1953 to 1978* (London, 1981). His reputation also rests on his adaptations on some of the books of *The Iliad*.

One of Italy's most famous Englishmen, the journalist and writer **Peter Nichols** (1928–1989) was born in Portsmouth and educated at Portsmouth Grammar School. He joined *The Times* in 1953, and, after a spell in Bonn, was made Rome correspondent in 1957, a position he held for thirty years. His writings included *The Politics of the Vatican* (1968) and *The*

Pope's Divisions (1981). *Italia, Italia* (1973) was his survey of the country which became his home.

Born on Hayling Island, the playwright **Simon Gray** (1936–2008) was educated at Portsmouth Grammar School and Westminster School. He wrote a number of novels, but enjoyed greater success writing for television, including adaptations of his own stage plays. His works for the theatre included *Wise Child* (1967), *Butley* (1971) and *Quartermaine's Terms* (1981). He was also a prolific diarist, with the pleasures of drinking and smoking a frequent theme.

Portsmouth-born playwright **Howard Brenton** (*b.* 1942) was educated at Chichester High School and Cambridge. His plays include *Magnificence* (1973), *Brassneck* (1973), *The Churchill Play* (1974), *Weapons of Happiness* (1976), *The Romans in Britain* (1980) and *Pravda* (1985).

Anglo-American iconoclast **Christopher Hitchens** lost his battle against cancer just before Christmas 2011. Author, critic and *bon vivant*, he was born in Portsmouth in 1949, the son of a commander in the Royal Navy. Never less than provocative, Hitchens placed himself at the forefront of public debate. *God Is Not Great: How Religion Poisons Everything* (2007) was among his most striking works. He maintained his crusading atheism until the end – though he did once comment: 'But I like surprises.' His obituary in *The Daily Telegraph* commented:

> *Over the course of his career the self-confessed contrarian gleefully picked fights with political opponents, Nobel Peace Prize winners and religious believers of all faiths. He fired his trademark put-downs and scathing critiques at figures such as Ronald Reagan, Bill Clinton and Mother Teresa.*

Goodnight Mister Tom author **Michelle Magorian** was born in Portsmouth on 6 November 1947. Made into a TV film starring the late John Thaw, the work won the 1982 Guardian Prize for British children's books with its tale of a London evacuee who strikes up an unlikely but moving friendship with the crusty old countryman with whom he is sent to live in order to escape the Blitz.

Portsmouth-born playwright **Nick Dear** (*b.* 1955) won a BAFTA award for his TV adaptation of Jane Austen's *Persuasion*. He also adapted Dostoevsky's *The Gambler* for Channel 4. Dear's stage plays include *Temptation* (1984), *The Art of Success* (1986) and *A Family Affair* (1988).

Multi-award-winning author and former Portsmouth resident **Neil Gaiman** declared himself 'gobsmacked, befuddled, delighted and baffled' in summer 2013 when a road in the city was named in his honour.

The lane, west of Canoe Lake, was called The Ocean at the End of the Lane, the title of his most recent novel. Gaiman's work includes the Sandman graphic novels, *Coraline*, *Stardust*, *American Gods* and two *Doctor Who* episodes.

Gaiman, who now lives in the US, was born in White Hart Lane, Portchester in 1960 and grew up in Purbook and then Southsea.

He commented: 'I lived in Portchester and Southsea until I was five. But my grandparents and much of my family were in Southsea, so I was back every school holiday and stayed as long as I could. I was even bar mitzvahed in the Portsmouth Synagogue.'

PORTSMOUTH CULTURE

Doctor Who

With vessels coming and going, Portsmouth is certainly used to travellers, but among its many visitors over the years is one who has surely clocked up the most miles of all: a traveller who routinely crosses the boundaries of time as well as space and is known only as the Doctor.

The BBC TV programme *Doctor Who*, which began in 1963, has used Portsmouth for location filming twice so far.

The first occasion was in 1971, when Jon Pertwee was the Time Lord, for a six-part adventure called *The Sea Devils*. This featured an underwater reptilian

race that had preceded humans on Earth and gone into hibernation to avoid a cosmic disaster that ultimately never happened. Millions of years later, the oversleeping creatures had been awakened and they wanted their planet back from mankind, which they viewed contemptuously as upstart apes.

Both Pertwee and producer Barry Letts had been in the Royal Navy, and since the Army and RAF had helped with previous *Doctor Who* stories it was felt that this would give the senior service an ideal opportunity to shine in the show. Seizing upon the invaluable PR potential, the navy went out of its way to provide equipment, bases and people.

Extensive filming took place in Portsmouth between 21 and 26 October 1971. The Fraser Gunnery Range at Eastney became the fictional shore base HMS *Seaspite*, while the deep-diving and submarine-rescue vessel HMS *Reclaim* plus No Man's Land Fort in the Solent were also used to great effect. Although Portsmouth wasn't specifically mentioned in the story, Southsea is clearly visible in the background, and one of the naval characters makes reference to the shore establishment HMS *Vernon* – now Gunwharf Quays.

Fast-forward to 1985 and we find the Doctor back in Portsmouth. This time, Colin Baker is in the title role and facing the Daleks, while Portsmouth is standing in for somewhere millions of miles away.

The two-part story *Revelation of the Daleks* needed a building that looked both funereal and futuristic to represent the cryogenic facility Tranquil Repose on the planet Necros, and the gleaming black edifice of IBM's UK headquarters at North Harbour was deemed ideal for this. The BBC used the exterior of the complex, shooting there on 9 January 1985, with huge pyramids being added in post-production.

The computer and technology services giant donated its filming fee to a special school in Portsmouth – Cliffdale Primary – which Baker visited to present the cheque.

The Sea Devils aired between 26 February and 1 April 1972, while *Revelation of the Daleks* was transmitted on 23 and 30 March 1985.

Twinning

The retraction of the armed forces from the Portsmouth area in the second half of the twentieth century was offset to an extent by the city's growing importance as a commercial ferry port, taking over from Southampton with shorter routes to mainland Europe. Portsmouth Continental Ferry Port offers ferry services to Caen, Cherbourg, St Malo and Le Havre in France; to the Channel Islands; and to Santander in Spain. The ferry port business has become a vital part of Portsmouth's economy.

The ferry has also helped strengthen the city's links with the continent. The ferry service between

Portsmouth and **Caen** made the two places natural twins. In 1987 documents were signed in Portsmouth Guildhall and in the *Hôtel de Ville*, Caen, formally declaring that the two cities would foster exchanges and meetings between their respective citizens in all fields of endeavour. The twinning has proved successful at all levels from school exchanges to art projects, from commercial links to sports tournaments. The friendship is renewed every year when the Lord Mayor of Portsmouth visits Caen for the D-Day commemoration ceremonies. The Mayor of Caen is similarly a regular visitor to Portsmouth.

Portsmouth is also twinned with **Duisburg** in Germany, the second oldest Anglo-German twinning. Duisburg is a city of more than 500,000 people in the North-Rhine Westphalia region, with the largest inland port in the world. Portsmouth City Council suggested a bond of friendship between the two cities as an act of reconciliation in the immediate aftermath of the Second World War. In 1950 the Lord Mayor and Lady Mayoress of Portsmouth (Sir Denis and Lady Peggy Daley) signed the Golden Book of Duisburg, and the twinning between Portsmouth and Duisburg was formalised. Since then, the twinning – as with Caen in more recent years – has flourished across a wide range of activities.

In addition to the official twinnings with Caen and Duisburg, Portsmouth enjoys sister links with Haifa, Israel; Maizuru, Japan; Portsmouth, Virginia; and Sydney, Australia. It also has friendship links with Lakewood, Colorado; Portsmouth, New Hampshire; and Zha Lai Te Qi, China.

Sticky Ends

Fate deals the cruellest hands. The people of Portsmouth have not been exempt.

The entire town of Portsmouth was held to account for the slaying of **Adam Moleyns**, administrator and Bishop of Chichester. Moleyns arrived in Portsmouth on 9 January 1450 where a mob dragged him from the Domus Dei, later the Royal Garrison Church, and murdered him on the beach nearby.

Some people believe there was a dispute over money he was carrying in payment to troops; some believe the troops blamed him for military losses in Normandy; others believe he was assassinated to order. Quite why he was killed will never be known, but the Church took out its anger on the whole population, excommunicating all the citizens of Portsmouth.

The *Oxford Dictionary of National Biography* describes Moleyns as 'one of the most respected of the few English humanist scholars of his day'; a man celebrated for his attempts to secure peace and for his wise counsel in the affairs of the realm.

Good looks and a sure instinct in matters of administration brought **George Villiers, first Duke of Buckingham** (1592–1628) significant admirers, not least James I. Buckingham became a royal favourite, but popularity with the king brought him much of the blame amongst the people for the king's unpopular policies. Buckingham's machinations abroad led the Commons to try to impeach him in 1626, and he was denounced, under Charles I, as the cause of all England's evils. John Felton, a naval lieutenant who had served under him, consequently felt it his duty to assassinate him and duly did so when Buckingham was in Portsmouth on matters of state. At 11 High Street, premises then known as the Spotted Dog, Felton stabbed him; Buckingham managed to cry 'villain' before dropping dead. His memorial nearby in Portsmouth Cathedral states:

> *While he was preparing armies a second time against the enemy, in this very town, fatal theatre of monstrous murder, where a new ocean overflows of blood and tears, he was struck down by the impious hand of a most accursed assassin on the twenty-third day of August in the year of our Lord 1628.*

The reality is that London rejoiced at the news. Personal enrichment and corruption were widely regarded as Buckingham's principal concerns. Felton was hanged at Tyburn on 29 November 1628; when his body was sent back to Portsmouth as an example, admiration was generally the reaction.

It's impossible not to feel a certain sympathy for **Admiral John Byng**, the man executed in Portsmouth – as Voltaire put it – 'to encourage the others'. In his *Candide*, Voltaire writes, '*Dans ce pays-*

ci, il est bon de tuer de temps en temps un amiral pour encourager les autres' – a rather scathing view of a British Admiralty which suggested an example had to be made every now and again simply to keep up standards. The unfortunate Byng (1704–1757) joined the navy at the age of thirteen and was a rear-admiral at the age of forty-one. However, when he was dispatched to protect Minorca against the French on the eve of the Seven Years' War (1756–1763), he came off worse and retreated to Gibraltar. He was recalled, court-martialled, sentenced to death and shot on the quarter-deck of the *Monarque* in Portsmouth Harbour. Contemporary accounts record his courage in his final moments.

It probably came as no consolation to James Aitken (1752–1777) that his gallows were the highest ever used in an execution in England. He was hanged from the mizzen mast of the *Arethusa*, which had been erected on Portsmouth Common especially for the occasion on a day which attracted crowds some 20,000 strong. To them all, he was better known as **John the Painter**, after the trade he exploited with such ghastly intent. Born in Edinburgh, Aitken drifted south into a life of crime in London. Briefly, he tried to make a new life for himself in Virginia, but soon returned to England where, to do his bit for the American revolutionary cause, he determined to destroy all six of the royal dockyards. Aitken secured slightly half-hearted American backing and even came up with his own incendiary device, using his professional knowledge to mix chemicals and paint solvents to explosive effect. In his first attack, he caused minor damage to the ropehouse in Portsmouth Dockyard in December 1776; his second attack caused rather more damage in Bristol the following month. After his capture, Aitken denied his guilt, changing his tune only after his conviction. His confession, dictated in prison, was published as *The Life of James Aitken* (1777).

It was a tragic way to go. **James Cranstoun**, the eighth Lord Cranstoun (*bap.* 1755, *d.* 1796), died after drinking cider which had been kept in a vessel lined with lead. He was buried in the Garrison Church at Portsmouth. A naval officer, he commanded the

64-gun *Belliqueux* and also the *Formidable* at the Battle of the Saintes (12 April 1782), an action which brought the destruction of the French West India squadron. Later commanding the *Bellerophon* off Point Penmarch on the west coast of Brittany, he and his comrades repulsed an attack by a French squadron – an action for which they received the thanks of Parliament.

The **Bounty** is a name synonymous with mutiny, and it was in Portsmouth that three of the mutineers paid the price for their rebellion. On 5 April 1789 the ship set sail to carry breadfruit seedlings from Tahiti to the West Indies; on 28 April, under the leadership of Fletcher Christian, part of the crew of 45 men mutinied. Whether the cause was dislike of the stern disciplinarian William Bligh who commanded them, or simply because the sailors had taken a liking to the women and other attractions of the South Sea Islands, is open to debate, but Bligh and the men loyal to him were cast adrift on an epic 3,600-mile journey to safety. The Admiralty sent HMS *Pandora* to Tahiti to bring back the mutineers for trial. Four of the mutineers were drowned when the *Pandora* was wrecked on the Great Barrier Reef. The remaining ten were court-martialled in Portsmouth. Three were sentenced to death and hanged.

Allen Francis Gardiner (1794–1851) entered the Royal Naval College, Portsmouth in May 1808 and served on various ships including HMS *Fortune* and HMS *Phoebe*, but it was the missionary life which was his true calling. In the face of political difficulties and native wars, he tried to set up Christian churches in Zululand, then spent five years working among the Indians of Chile. He distributed Bibles to the Indian population in Bolivia and in 1847 published *A Voice from South America*. His work in Tierra del Fuego, however, was to end in tragedy. He landed at Picton Island on 5 December 1850 with sufficient supplies for six months. The locals were hostile; further provisions failed to get through; and Gardiner and his fellow missionaries died one by one of starvation.

The last moments and the death of **Lionel Kenneth Philip 'Buster' Crabb** look likely to remain one of Portsmouth's most gruesome secrets. In April 1956, the Russian cruiser *Ordzhonikidze* was in Portsmouth Harbour carrying the Soviet leaders Bulganin and Khrushchev to Britain for a formal visit. Crabb (1909–1956), a naval and MI6 frogman, entered the water three times to investigate the ship's design, the third time never to return. More than a year later, a headless body – later identified as Crabb – was found in Chichester Harbour. Had he been killed by a secret Soviet underwater weapon? Or maybe the body wasn't his – despite the official identification. Some people believe he defected to the Russians, or was captured and brainwashed. Rather more sinisterly, it is possible that he was murdered by MI6. More prosaically, it may simply be that Crabb was unfit for duty and paid the price. Will we ever know exactly what happened? Almost certainly not.

And the one that got away...

Rose Robinson, licensee of the John Barleycorn in Portsmouth, was strangled during the night of 28–

29 November 1943 as she counted the day's takings in her bedroom above the pub. Nearly a month after the murder, **Harold Loughans** was picked up by the police in London and admitted he had 'done a murder job in Hampshire'. Crucial in all that subsequently happened was a deformity to his right hand which left him effectively with four half-fingers alongside an intact thumb. Forensic pathologist Keith Simpson, however, saw this as no reason to suppose him incapable of the murder.

However, at the trial in Winchester in March 1944, Loughans claimed the police had fabricated his confessions; the jury failed to agree on a verdict; and a retrial took place at the Old Bailey two weeks later. Here the defence played its trump card: the eminent pathologist Sir Bernard Spilsbury. On the evidence of shaking Loughans' hand at Brixton prison, Sir Bernard pronounced:

> *I do not believe he could strangle anyone with that hand.*
>
> *FORTY YEARS OF MURDER*, PROFESSOR KEITH SIMPSON (GRAFTON, 1980)

Loughans was acquitted and escaped the gallows. But that was not the end of the matter. In 1963, he walked into the offices of *The People* newspaper and said:

They tell me I have cancer and haven't long to live. Before I die I want to make a confession. I want to say I done that job. I did kill the woman in the public house in Portsmouth.

IBID.

Ghosts

Think of all the misdeeds, the killings, the crimes, the horrors, the assassinations, the piracy, the press-ganging and the delinquency which have gone on in the city, much of it fuelled by alcohol or by poverty in times of stress, times of war. It is surely no surprise that Portsmouth is a city overflowing with tales of ghosts, ghouls and things that go bump in the night.

Portsmouth's Wymering Manor is proud to count itself among the country's most haunted buildings, a sure favourite with ghost hunters who will be disappointed to come away with anything less than a little look at the spectral nun whose hands are said to drip with blood, or a glimpse of the embalmed girl with a ghastly painted face.

You can take your pick across the city: a murdered sailor on the site of the former Blue Posts Inn or maybe a detachment of First World War soldiers in Hayling Avenue. Or you could search out the ghost of frogman Buster Crabb at the Keppel's Head Hotel. Not far away, the Duke of Buckingham is said in some senses never to have left the Spotted Dog inn where he was dispatched to meet his maker. Elsewhere, a murdered Victorian barmaid is said to roam.

But my favourite story will always be the one my paternal grandmother, Kathleen 'Kit' Hewitt, used to love to tell us. I can hear her telling the tale even now, nearly thirty years after her death; how I wish we had thought to capture it on tape.

Kit's mother was a young woman walking home through Old Portsmouth one night in the late nineteenth century. Alone and vulnerable, she realised she was walking towards a group of sailors, rough, ready, rowdy and most definitely the worse for wear. Fear seized her, but moments later a horse and carriage pulled up beside her on the cobbled street.

A tall, smartly dressed man descended and held out his riding whip in front of the drunken sailors, allowing my great-grandmother to pass by unmolested. She hurried on gratefully, and it was only once the danger had passed that she realised – she hadn't heard the horse and carriage pull up beside on her on Old Portsmouth's cobbled street. And nor had she heard it leave.

Spinnaker Tower – a Symbol of Modern Portsmouth

Taller than Big Ben, the **Spinnaker Tower** soars 170 metres above the waterfront at Gunwharf Quays, a symbol of the confidence of modern Portsmouth. Yet the whole project got off to the worst possible start.

Portsmouth's Spinnaker Tower ran significantly over budget and straight into angry wrangling about contracts and critical reports. Construction finally got underway in 2001, two years after its promised opening – a delay so spectacular that the Tower's intended name had to be dropped. There was no longer any point calling it the Portsmouth Millennium Tower.

And then, just as everyone concerned hoped to put the problems behind them, the external lift stuck on the very day it opened, trapping distinguished guests in full public view for an hour and a half, suspended for all to see. Abseiling engineers had to rescue them on a humiliating day for a project which seemed destined never to get anything right.

But what a transformation we have seen since. Visible for miles around, the Spinnaker Tower has established itself as an important symbol of twenty-first-century Portsmouth and a much-loved feature of the Portsmouth skyline – distinctions which are a tribute to the beauty and elegance of its design.

The substitute name is undoubtedly the better name, one which reflects both Portsmouth's maritime history and the design of the tower itself, with its representation of sails billowing in the wind. Despite weighing more than 30,000 tonnes, it offers a remarkable impression of grace and poise. Not surprisingly, it has become a major attraction, with two million visitors enjoying the view since its rather fraught opening in October 2005.

The Tower's three viewing platforms offer very nearly a 360-degree panorama. From the top you can look east or west for a superb view along the coast; you can look south across the Solent towards the Isle of Wight, and north towards Portchester Castle, the Roman settlement from which Portsmouth sprang. On a clear day you can see for 23 miles.

But maybe it's best not to gaze into the distance. Maybe it's better to look straight down to enjoy the view of Portsmouth itself, an endlessly fascinating city which has shaped the maritime history of our nation.

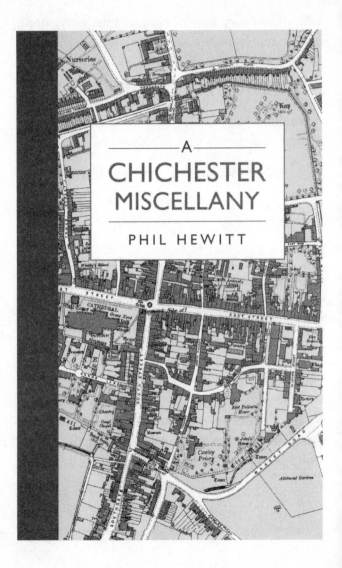

A

CHICHESTER
MISCELLANY

PHIL HEWITT

A CHICHESTER MISCELLANY

Phil Hewitt

ISBN: 978 1 84953 379 9   Hardback   £9.99

Home to a magnificent Norman Cathedral, Chichester was created by the Romans and developed as a thriving market town in the Middle Ages. The Georgians added an array of splendid buildings which still enhance the city today, and during recent decades Chichester has emerged as a major centre for the arts, with an enviable reputation. In this captivating compendium of fascinating facts and quirky true stories, Phil Hewitt reveals the intriguing history and the hidden delights of one of our best-loved cathedral cities.

'Full of oohs and aahs... To read things about where you reside is always enlightening, but the bottom line is that this book is fun'

CHRISTOPHER TIMOTHY

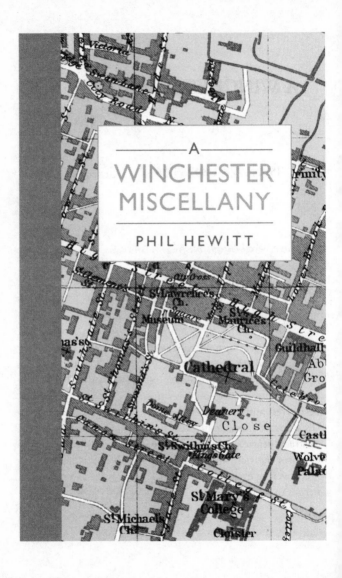

—— A ——
WINCHESTER
MISCELLANY

PHIL HEWITT

A WINCHESTER MISCELLANY

Phil Hewitt

ISBN: 978 1 84953 464 2   Hardback   £9.99

You have here history, and you have it in a form that charms the eye and refreshes the spirit.

PRIME MINISTER STANLEY BALDWIN, ON RECEIVING THE
FREEDOM OF WINCHESTER, JULY 1928

Winchester is a city with a wealth of enigma and history; the place where a cake-burning king established a nation; a city where a queen encased herself in a coffin to escape besieging forces; the final resting place of one of Britain's best-loved authors; a host to diverse events from one of the UK's largest farmer's markets to the longest-running festival of street theatre. In this fascinating and informative guide, Phil explores the rich story of the city and brings Winchester to life, covering everything from its legends to its kings, from its heroes to its villains.

KEEP ON RUNNING

THE HIGHS
& LOWS OF A
MARATHON ADDICT

Phil Hewitt

KEEP ON RUNNING
The Highs and Lows of a Marathon Addict

Phil Hewitt

ISBN: 978 1 84953 236 5   Paperback   £8.99

Phil Hewitt, who has completed over 20 marathons in conditions ranging from blistering heat to snow and ice, in locations from Berlin to New York, sets a cracking pace in this light-hearted account of his adventures on the road. This story of an ordinary guy's addiction to running marathons looks at the highs and lows, the motivation that keeps you going when your body is crying out to stop, and tries to answer the ultimate question, 'Why do you do it?'

'This is a wonderful and frank view of a first-time-marathoner-turned-running-addict. Phil shares the pitfalls and emotions that running a marathon for the first time evoke and how running can grab you and draw you back for more'

LIZ YELLING, DOUBLE OLYMPIAN AND COMMONWEALTH BRONZE MEDALLIST

'For those of us fitting running in between job, family and everything else life has to throw at us, this is definitely a book you will make a connection with'

MEN'S RUNNING MAGAZINE, NOVEMBER 2012

Have you enjoyed this book?
If so, why not write a review on
your favourite website?

If you're interested in finding out more
about our books, find us on Facebook
at **Summersdale Publishers** and follow
us on Twitter at **@Summersdale**.

Thanks very much for buying
this Summersdale book.

www.summersdale.com

Priddys Hard

Landing Stage

Lake

Dock

Factory
Smithy

Slips

Burrow
Observatory Island

Royal
Dock Yard

Filling
Basin

Royal Clarence
Victualling Yard

South Jetty

Watering
Island

PO

National Schools

King S.

Clarence
Sq.

Portsmouth
Harbour Sta

North S.

PORT

The
Green

High Street

Steam Launch
Ferry

Market Ho.

Upper South S.

Floating Bridge
(Ferry)

Alms Ho.

Chapel L.

Trinity Ch.

Illustrious Hard

The Point

Coast Guard
Sta.

aslar

Gosport
Bridge

Toll Bar

Lake

Blockhouse
Fort

Point
Batter

Broa

PO

Vie